Leckie×Leckie

Scotland's leading educational publishers

#1 FOR REVISION

National 5
PHYSICS
SUCCESS GUIDE

N5 **PHYSICS** *SUCCESS GUIDE*

John Taylor

© 2014 Leckie & Leckie Ltd
Cover © ink-tank

001/05052014

10 9 8 7 6 5 4 3 2 1

ISBN 9780007504701

Published by
Leckie & Leckie Ltd
An imprint of HarperCollins*Publishers*
Westerhill Road, Bishopbriggs, Glasgow, G64 2QT
T: 0844 576 8126   F: 0844 576 8131
leckieandleckie@harpercollins.co.uk   www.leckieandleckie.co.uk

Special thanks to
Jill Laidlaw (copy edit and proofread)
Donna Cole (proofread)
Jennifer Richards (proofread)
Alistair Coats (proofread)
Ian Mitchell (content review)
QBS (layout)

Printed in Italy by Lego S.P.A.

A CIP Catalogue record for this book is available from the British Library.

Acknowledgements

Images from the following pages are © Shutterstock.com: P13, P16, P17, P36, P42, P44, P60, P61, P62, P63, P64, P65, P78, P84, P89, P90, P91, P96, P99, P100, P110, P114, P120, P121, P123, P124, P126

Contents

Unit 1: Electricity and energy

Unit 2: Waves and radiation

Contents

Unit 3: Dynamics and space

Introduction

Physics

- Studying physics provides us with a deep understanding of our world and its place in the Universe.
- An understanding of physics is fundamental to a deeper understanding of all science.
- Physics studies the energy sources we need for everyday life through to the latest developments in the exploration of space and, in between, all the many applications that have been developed as a result of the discoveries of the laws of physics.
- Physics has been developed as a result of practical experimentation and theoretical thinking, and you will develop these skills as you do this physics course.
- In scale, physics ranges from the study of the smallest parts of the atom through to the size of the Universe itself.
- Modern technology exists and develops as a result of our understanding of physics.

National 5 Physics

The National 5 Physics course has three main units. The key areas of these units are:

- **Electricity and energy:** conservation of energy, electrical charge carriers and electric fields, potential difference (voltage), practical electrical and electronic circuits, Ohm's law, electrical power, specific heat capacity, gas laws and the kinetic model.
- **Waves and radiation:** wave parameters and behaviours, the electromagnetic spectrum, light and nuclear radiation.
- **Dynamics and space:** velocity and displacement, velocity-time graphs, acceleration, Newton's laws, projectile motion, space exploration and cosmology.

National 5 Physics assessment: unit assessment

To gain National 5 Physics, you must pass all of the units. There are three assessment tasks for each of the units.

Task 1

This is a scientific report of an experiment or practical investigation.

You should:

- Start with a plan, for example, after the title you should include: an aim, a dependent and independent variable, variables to be kept constant, measurements/observations to be made, resources used, a diagram of the method (including safety considerations if appropriate).
- Follow your procedures safely.
- Make and record observations/measurements correctly.
- Present your results (with any repeats, averages) in an appropriate format, for example, table, line graph, chart, key, diagram or summary.
- Draw a valid conclusion (refer to your aim).
- Evaluate your experimental procedures, give a reason and suggest an improvement.

Task 2

This is a short scientific report of a research investigation.

You should:

- Describe an application – include the physics of the application.
- Describe the physics issue in terms of the effect on the environment/society.

Task 3

This is a set of questions.

You should:

- Make accurate statements.
- Solve problems.

National 5 Physics assessment: course assessment

The final course assessment is graded A–D. There is a question paper worth 80 marks and an assignment worth 20 marks, making a total of 100 marks.

Question paper

The question paper will actually show 110 marks! The question paper has 20 marks of Objective Test questions followed by restricted and extended response questions showing 90 marks but these will be scaled by the SQA to 60 marks. The total is now 80 marks! You need to complete this paper in 2 hours.

Marks will be awarded for applying knowledge and understanding, for applying scientific inquiry, scientific analytical thinking and problem solving skills.

A data sheet containing relevant data and formulae will be provided.

Assignment

This assignment requires you to apply skills, knowledge and understanding to investigate a relevant topic in physics (from one or more of the key areas of the course) and its effect on the environment and/or society.

You will need to spend most time in the **research stage**. Here you will decide on your aim and gather and prepare scientific data. You will need to use, describe and explain at least two sources.

You will then need to present your information during a **communication stage**. Use a structured report with a suitable title and headings. A good report should also include:

- The aim of the investigation (the aspect that you investigated).
- The application and the effect on the environment and/or society.
- Sources of data/information (stating how relevant and reliable).
- Relevant information from the sources (raw data, calculations, graphs, tables, etc.)
- Your processing and presentation of data/information (graphs, tables, charts, diagrams, etc. with suitable scales, headings, units and labels). Compare the data.
- A valid conclusion.
- Your description of the physics knowledge and understanding and explanation of its relevance.

All of the course assessment evidence will be submitted to the SQA for external marking.

General information

In order to do well in the assessments you will need to revise knowledge and understanding as well as the practical skills developed during your course.

There are variations in how or when you can be assessed. This introduction has been written as a general guide and you should confirm with your centre that you have the latest advice. You should also be issued with detailed advice for candidates at appropriate times.

You will find traffic lights throughout this book to help you assess how well you understand each section.

GOT IT? ☐ ☐ ☐

Study hard and success will follow.

Essential equations

$E_p = mgh$

$E_k = \dfrac{1}{2}mv^2$

$Q = It$

$V = IR$

$R_T = R_1 + R_2 + \dots$

$\dfrac{1}{R_1} = \dfrac{1}{R_1} + \dfrac{1}{R_2} + \dots$

$V_2 = \left(\dfrac{R_2}{R_1 + R_2}\right)V_s$

$\dfrac{V_1}{V_2} = \dfrac{R_1}{R_2}$

$P = \dfrac{E}{t}$

$P = IV$

$P = I^2R$

$P = \dfrac{V^2}{R}$

$E_h = cm\Delta T$

$P = \dfrac{F}{A}$

$\dfrac{pV}{T} = \text{constant}$

$p_1 V_1 = p_2 V_2$

$\dfrac{p_1}{T_1} = \dfrac{p_2}{T_2}$

$\dfrac{V_1}{T_1} = \dfrac{V_2}{T_2}$

$d = vt$

$v = f\lambda$

$T = \dfrac{1}{f}$

$A = \dfrac{N}{t}$

$D = \dfrac{E}{m}$

$H = Dw_R$

$\dot{H} - \dfrac{H}{t}$

$s = vt$

$d = \bar{v}t$

$s = \bar{v}t$

$a = \dfrac{v - u}{t}$

$W = mg$

$F = ma$

$E_w = Fd$

$E_h = ml$

Additional equations worth learning

Series circuits:

$V = V_1 + V_2 + V_3$

$I = I_1 = I_2 = I_3$

Parallel circuits:

$V = V_1 = V_2 = V_3$

$I = I_1 + I_2 + I_3$

TOP TIP

Learn equations: it will save you time in the exams.

Data and relations

Physics to learn	Identify data and equations.
Success guide	You are able to find the required data or equations from a list of tables or list.

Essential data

Speed of light in materials

Material	Speed (ms^{-1})
Air	$3 \cdot 0 \times 10^8$
Carbon dioxide	$3 \cdot 0 \times 10^8$
Diamond	$1 \cdot 2 \times 10^8$
Glass	$2 \cdot 0 \times 10^8$
Glycerol	$2 \cdot 1 \times 10^8$
Water	$2 \cdot 3 \times 10^8$

Gravitational field strengths

Location	Gravitational field strength on the surface (kg^{-1})
Earth	9·8
Jupiter	23.0
Mars	3·7
Mercury	3·7
Moon	1·6
Neptune	11.0
Saturn	9·0
Sun	270.0
Uranus	8·7
Venus	8·9

Specific latent heat of fusion of materials

Material	Specific latent heat of fusion (J kg^{-1})
Alcohol	$0 \cdot 99 \times 10^5$
Aluminium	$3 \cdot 95 \times 10^5$
Carbon dioxide	$1 \cdot 80 \times 10^5$
Copper	$2 \cdot 05 \times 10^5$
Iron	$2 \cdot 67 \times 10^5$
Lead	$0 \cdot 25 \times 10^5$
Water	$3 \cdot 34 \times 10^5$

Specific latent heat of vaporisation of materials

Material	Specific latent heat of vaporisation (J kg^{-1})
Alcohol	$11 \cdot 2 \times 10^5$
Carbon dioxide	$3 \cdot 77 \times 10^5$
Glycerol	$8 \cdot 30 \times 10^5$
Turpentine	$2 \cdot 90 \times 10^5$
Water	$22 \cdot 6 \times 10^5$

Speed of sound in materials

Material	Speed (ms^{-1})
Aluminium	5200
Air	340
Bone	4100
Carbon dioxide	270
Glycerol	1900
Muscle	1600
Steel	5200
Tissue	1500
Water	1500

Melting and boiling points of materials

Material	Melting point (°C)	Boiling point (°C)
Alcohol	−98	65
Aluminium	660	2470
Copper	1077	2567
Glycerol	18	290
Lead	328	1737
Iron	1537	2737

Specific heat capacity of materials

Material	Specific heat capacity (J kg^{-1} °C^{-1})
Alcohol	2350
Aluminium	902
Copper	386
Glass	500
Ice	2100
Iron	480
Lead	128
Oil	2130
Water	4180

Radiation weighting factors

Type of radiation	Radiation weighting factor
alpha	20
beta	1
fast neutrons	10
gamma	1
slow neutrons	3

Matter and energy

Physics to learn	How to consider the terms matter, mass and energy.
Success guide	You will be able to give typical examples.

At the heart of physics

Physics involves the study of **matter** and **energy**. But what are these quantities? When we try to understand our universe, we gather information from matter and energy. Galaxies, stars, planets, humans, animals and molecules are all made of matter. These objects can interact by exchanging energy such as heat, light, sound and kinetic energy.

Energy cannot be created or destroyed, it can only be changed or transformed from one form to another. This is known as the **law of conservation**.

Matter and mass

Matter is usually the general name for the substance from which an object is made. Matter will have mass and volume.

Small particles – such as atoms – and sub-atomic particles – such as protons, neutrons and electrons – are the building blocks of matter.

Matter can exist in different states, e.g. solid, liquid, gas or plasma.

Mass defines the amount of matter in an object, measured in kilograms.

Energy

What are the different forms of energy?

Potential energy

This is the energy that is or can be stored in an object. This energy has the potential to do work e.g. a coiled spring can turn a clock, or the stretched rubber in a catapult can release a projectile.

- **Gravitational potential energy.** The energy an object has when it has been raised through the gravitational field. This energy will not just make an object fall towards the planet, but will make it accelerate, e.g. a skydiver jumping from a plane.

- **Chemical potential energy.** The energy stored within the bonds of atoms and molecules of a substance. A battery has chemical potential energy.

Kinetic energy

The energy of moving objects is called kinetic energy.

A car and its passengers need a lot of energy to get moving. They have gained kinetic energy. The car would keep moving if there was no friction to overcome during the journey. When brakes are applied the kinetic energy changes into a different form of energy: mainly heat energy and a little sound energy.

Heat energy

When something heats up, it is said to have gained heat energy. All atoms in any substance vibrate slightly, providing they are above absolute zero (0 kelvin). Increasing a substance's heat energy causes the atoms in that substance to vibrate faster.

Sound energy

Sound energy also occurs when atoms or molecules in a substance vibrate. The energy is passed from molecule to molecule, travelling through the substance (gas, liquid or solid) as a wave. A tuning fork or loudspeaker sends vibrations through the air. Sound energy cannot travel through a vacuum e.g. space, as sound needs a medium to travel through.

Light energy

Light is a wave of energy and is part of the electromagnetic spectrum. Light energy can travel through space.

Electrical energy

Electrical charges moving around a circuit are doing work. The charges move slowly but electrical energy passes through the charges at virtually the speed of light.

Nuclear energy

This is a type of stored energy that exists in the electrical bonds between particles of the nucleus in an atom.

TOP TIP

Energy is measured in Joules (J).

Quick Test 1

1. Name **two** things that matter will have.
2. What is the unit of mass?
3. List **five** types of energy.
4. List **five** emitters of energy.
5. Research uses of energy.

Potential energy, kinetic energy and conservation

Physics to learn	Identify energy changes, derive potential and kinetic energy equations.
Success guide	Select energy equations to use where energy is transferred.

Energy transfers

Energy can transfer from one form to another.
- The sun transfers nuclear energy to heat and light energy.
- A candle transfers chemical energy to heat and light energy.
- A battery transfers chemical energy to electrical energy.
- A light bulb transfers electrical energy to light energy.

Important equations

In Unit 3 (Dynamics and space) we find that the equations for the weight of an object and the work done are:

Weight, $W = mg$ and work done, $E_w = Fd$.

Where W = weight, m = mass (in kg) and g = gravitational field strength (measured in ms^{-2} and usually defined as 9.8 ms^{-2} on Earth).

Potential energy

To lift an object up through the gravitational field of the planet we need to do work. We have to exert a force that is equal to the weight of the object for the distance equal to the height the object is raised.

This work is transferred to the object as gravitational potential energy.

The equation for calculating gravitational potential energy is found as follows:

Potential energy gain = Work done

$E_p = E_w$

$E_p = Fd$ (force × distance)

$E_p = mg × d$ (mass × gravity [the force needed] × distance [the change in height])

TOP TIP

$E_p = mgh$ can give an increase or decrease in potential energy.

So:

Potential energy = mass × gravity × change in height

$$E_p = mgh$$

Where:

- E_p is measured in joules
- m is measured in kg
- g is measured in ms^{-2} (g = 9.8 ms^{-2} on earth)
- h is measured in m

A forklift truck has lifted a 450 kg box by 5 m up to a shelf.

The gain in potential energy,

$$E_p = mgh$$
$$= 450 \times 9.8 \times 5$$
$$= 22\,050\,J$$

Whenever we raise a mass up through the gravitational field we do work. The mass stores this as a gain in potential energy.

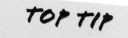

TOP TIP

Always check the units in every part of a question. If a quantity is given to you in g, you'll need to convert it to kg. If a distance is provided in cm, you will need to convert it to m.

TOP TIP

Energy is a scalar quantity with no direction.

Kinetic energy

Kinetic energy is the energy that moving objects have. They have gained this energy while accelerating. Work is being done by applying a force for a distance while accelerating the object.

Work done: $E_w = F\,d$

$$= mad$$

$$= m\left(\frac{v-u}{t}\right)\left(\frac{1}{2}vt\right)$$

$F = ma$

$$a = \frac{v-u}{t} \quad d = \frac{1}{2}vt$$

$u = 0$ and t cancels

so $\boxed{E_k = \frac{1}{2}mv^2}$

d = area under a v/t graph $= \frac{1}{2}vt$

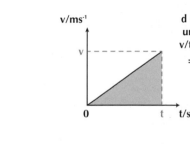

elastic bands mask light-gate interface computer or timer vehicle air blower air track

This air track vehicle is accelerated by the energy stored in the elastic bands. The vehicle gains kinetic energy.

The light gate is connected to a computer, which measures the **velocity**.

1. If the vehicle's mass is doubled, twice the energy (double the number of bands) is needed to get the same velocity. The experiment shows:

   Kinetic energy varies proportionately with mass: $E_K \propto m$

2. To get the vehicle to double its velocity requires four times the energy (number of elastics). The experiment shows:

   Kinetic energy varies proportionately to velocity squared $E_K \propto v^2$

- The kinetic energy depends on mass, e.g. a car and a lorry are going at the same speed – the lorry has more mass so it will take more work to stop. The more massive lorry has more kinetic energy.

- The kinetic energy depends on the square of the velocity, e.g. imagine two identical cars, one going twice as fast as the other; $2^2 = 4$. The faster car will have four times the kinetic energy. It will take four times as much work to stop. In a crash, there will be four times as much energy to do damage! How much more energy will a vehicle need to become three times as fast? $3^2 = 9$ times!

Example

A 1000 kg car is going at 30 ms^{-1} (70 mph). How much energy will be needed to stop it?

$$E_K = \frac{1}{2}\,mv^2 = \frac{1}{2}\,1000\,(30^2) = 500 \times 900 = 450\,000\,J.$$

Conservation of energy

Energy is never created or destroyed – just changed from one form to another. We can use this principle, known as the conservation of energy, to predict the velocity reached by the cars at the bottom of this rollercoaster.

Assume:

$$E_{P\,loss} = E_{K\,gain}$$

$$mgh = \frac{1}{2}\,mv^2$$

Quick Test 2

1. Calculate the gain in potential energy when a 3 kg bag is lifted onto a 2 m high shelf.

2. Calculate the potential energy a bow has when it is pulled back 0.2 m and held with a force of 50 N. (Hint: an extra step is needed here!)

3. A diver goes off a 6 m high board. Calculate the entry speed.

Energy, power and efficiency

Physics to learn	Energy and power relationship, explaining efficiency.
Success guide	You can select and use the correct energy equations and describe and explain energy loss situations. You can also use the correct efficiency equation.

Energy and power

Power is the rate of doing work or the work done in unit time (1 s).

Power is the rate of transferring energy or the energy transferred in unit time (1 s).

$$\text{power} = \frac{\text{work done}}{\text{time}}$$

$$\text{power} = \frac{\text{energy}}{\text{time}}$$

$$P = \frac{E}{t}$$

Power is measured in watts (W), $1\,W = 1\,J\,s^{-1}$

Re-arranging this equation can give the energy transferred: $E = Pt$ or the time: $t = \dfrac{E}{P}$

Energy 'loss', the great escape!

When a moving vehicle is stopped, the kinetic energy of the vehicle is mainly transformed to heat by the brakes. This heat energy will escape to the surroundings. Any energy that escapes as heat is hard to recover. It is usual to say the energy is 'lost'.

A skier is at the top of a 600 m high hill. She skis to the bottom, where she reaches a speed of $15\,ms^{-1}$. If her mass was 66 kg, how much energy was lost because of **friction** during the descent?

Her **potential energy** lost: $E_p = mgh = 66 \times 9.8 \times 600 = 388\,080$ J.

Her **kinetic energy** gained: $E_k = \frac{1}{2}\,mv^2 = \frac{1}{2} \times 66 \times 15^2 = 7425$ J.

We can see that this skier has used the force of friction to prevent her accelerating to too high a speed. Of her potential energy, $380\,655$ J has transferred to heat, and possibly a little sound.

From **conservation of energy:**
potential energy $\rightarrow$ kinetic energy + heat energy + sound energy.

Efficiency

In systems that convert energy from one type to another (such as power stations), energy is always lost to the surroundings. Energy escapes – usually as heat – and cannot be put back. The heat is regarded as waste energy.

Efficiency measures how much of the **total energy input** is kept as **useful output**.

Efficiency can be expressed as a percentage. This will always be less than 100%.

$$\text{percentage efficiency} = \frac{\text{useful energy output}}{\text{total energy input}} \times 100$$

$$\text{percentage efficiency} = \frac{\text{useful power output}}{\text{total power input}} \times 100$$

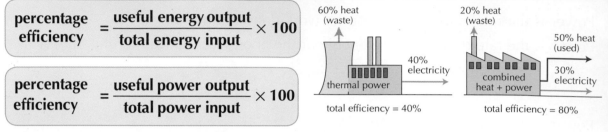

60% heat (waste)
40% electricity
thermal power
total efficiency = 40%

20% heat (waste)
50% heat (used)
30% electricity
combined heat + power
total efficiency = 80%

Energy transfers and losses

Example 1

A crane lifts a load of bricks of mass 1200 kg onto a building of height 12 m. The carrier itself has a mass of 300 kg.

What minimum power must the motor of the lift develop to lift the bricks in 15 s?

Work done = potential energy gained ($g = 9.8\,\text{N}\,\text{kg}^{-1}$)

$E_p = mgh = 1500 \times 9.8 \times 12 = 176\,400\,\text{J}$

$\text{Power, } P = \dfrac{E}{t} = \dfrac{176\,400}{15} = 11\,760\,\text{W}$

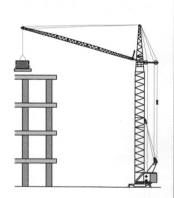

Example 2

A car of mass 800 kg, travelling at $20\,\text{ms}^{-1}$, is brought to rest in 40 s. Calculate the amount of power needed to achieve this.

Work done = kinetic energy lost

$E_K = \dfrac{1}{2}\,mv^2 = \dfrac{1}{2} \times 800 \times 20^2 = 160\,000\,\text{J}.$

$\text{Power, } P = \dfrac{E}{t} = \dfrac{160\,000}{40} = 4000\,\text{W or 4kW}.$

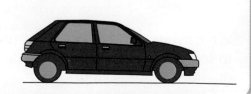

Example 3

A microwave supplies 800 J of energy to food for every 1500 J of energy it takes in. What is the efficiency of this machine?

$$\text{percentage efficiency} = \frac{\text{useful } E_o}{\text{total } E_i} \times 100$$

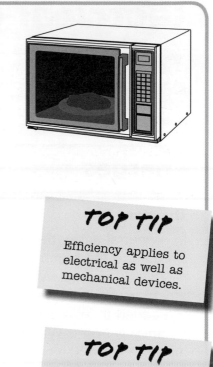

$$= \frac{800}{1500} \times 100 = 53\%$$

Example 4

> **TOP TIP**
>
> Efficiency applies to electrical as well as mechanical devices.

In a 60 W filament lamp only 9 W is converted to light. The rest goes to heat. How efficient is this lamp?

$$\text{percentage efficiency} = \frac{\text{useful } P_o}{\text{total } P_i} \times 100$$

$$= \frac{9}{60} \times 100 = 15\%$$

> **TOP TIP**
>
> Efficiency is always less than 100%. We cannot get more out than we put in!

Quick Test 3

1. What is the basic unit of time?
2. A dog pulls a sledge for 1500 m using a force of 50 N. Calculate the work done and calculate the dog's average power if it takes 10 minutes to pull the sledge that distance.
3. A 2 kW motor pulls a load of 3000 N 8 m. How long does it take?
4. How efficient is a machine that takes in 24 000 J and produces 8000 J of useful energy?
5. A machine that is 70% efficient has an input power of 360 W. Calculate the output power.
6. If the output power from a 40% efficient machine is 2400 W, what is the input power?

Electrical charge and fields

Physics to learn	How to describe charge carriers, electrostatic effects and electric current.
Success guide	You can use the relationship between charge and current.

Charges

TOP TIP

Protons and neutrons cannot normally leave an atom. Electrons are much smaller and can be easily stripped from the outermost shell of electrons in an atom.

The atom:

In a neutral atom, the number of protons is equal to the number of electrons and so the atom has no overall charge. When electrons either leave or are added to an atom, this balance is upset. When an atom **gains** electrons it becomes negatively charged. When it **loses** electrons it becomes **positively** charged.

An atom has a nucleus surrounded by shells of electrons.

The **electrons** are found in shells around the **nucleus**.

The **nucleus** is found at the centre of the **atom** and contains **neutrons** and **protons**.

Conductors and insulators

In a conductor, electrons are free to move.

In an insulator, electrons are not free to move as they are all bound in the atom.

Good conductors are metals (e.g. gold, silver, copper and aluminium), and carbon.

Insulators are usually non-metal, e.g. pvc, polythene, wood, rubber and paper.

Electrostatics

Rubbing two insulators together can electrically charge them by transferring electrons (negative charges) between them through friction. To make objects negatively or positively charged, electrons have to be added/removed.

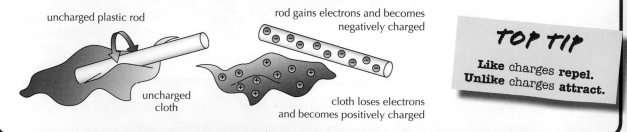

uncharged plastic rod

uncharged cloth

rod gains electrons and becomes negatively charged

cloth loses electrons and becomes positively charged

TOP TIP

Like charges **repel.**
Unlike charges **attract.**

Electric charge

The electron is extremely small. Electrons carry a negative charge.

Electric charge is measured in coulombs (C).

The charge of an electron is 1.6×10^{-19} C.

In an electric circuit we do not measure the number of electrons flowing in the circuit but the quantity of charge.

Electric current

When charges, e.g. electrons, flow we have an electric current.

Current is the rate at which charge flows and is the amount of charge transferred in unit time (1 s).

$$I = \frac{Q}{t} \qquad Q = It$$

Current (I) is measured in amperes (A).

Charge (Q) is measured in coulombs (C).

Time (t) is measured in seconds (s).

For example, 6 C passes a point in 2 minutes. What is the value of the current?

$$I = \frac{Q}{t} = \frac{6}{2 \times 60} = \frac{6}{120} = 0.05 \text{ A}$$

> **TOP TIP**
>
> Current does not flow. Current is a measure of the quantity of charge flowing.

Measuring current

An ammeter is placed in line (in series) with the circuit.

$I = 2$ A. This means 2 C of charge flows through the bulb every 1 s.

How much charge flowed when there was a current of 15 μA in a wire for 3 hours?

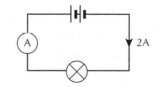

$Q = It = 15 \times 10^{-6} \times (3 \times 60 \times 60) = 0.162 = 0.16$ C

> **TOP TIP**
>
> Do not use amps or secs in your answers – they are not allowed. Instead, learn to use the symbols A and s.

Quick Test 4

1. What type of charge is on:

    (a) a proton   (b) a neutron   (c) an electron?

2. What type of charge flows in electric circuits?

3. A proton and electron are close together. Will they attract or repel?

4. Why are electrical wires made of copper and covered in plastic?

5. A circuit current is 0.5 A. Calculate how much charge passes in 3 minutes.

Potential difference (voltage)

Physics to learn	Electric fields, voltage and potential difference.
Success guide	Explain how charge experiences a force, describe and measure voltages.

Electric field

The region around an electric charge is an **electric field**.

In an electric field, an electric charge experiences a force.

Force causes acceleration, and work done by the field on charges creates kinetic energy in the charges. The field lines show the direction in which a positive charge will move, so in a circuit electrons flow against the field lines.

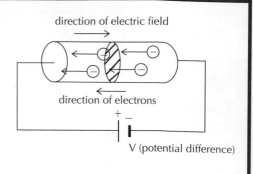

Circuit symbols

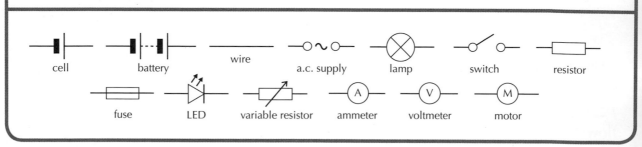

Voltage

The voltage of a supply is a measure of the energy given to the charges in a circuit.

The voltage (or potential difference, p.d.) across a component is a measure of the energy given out by charges as they go through the component.

Voltage (V) or p.d. is measured in volts (V).

A voltage of 1 V means 1 J of electrical energy is changing into other forms every time 1 C of charge passes through.

In this circuit:

- the charges have gained energy from the cell
- the lamp changes some of the electrical energy into light
- the resistor changes some of the electrical energy into heat
- the motor changes some of the electrical energy into kinetic energy.

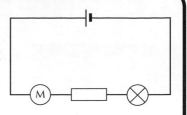

Measuring voltage

A voltmeter is placed across (in parallel with) the component being measured, e.g. a battery.

Number of cells	Voltage (V)
1	1.5
2	3.0
3	4.5
4	6.0

A voltage reading of 4.5 V here means 4.5 J of energy is being supplied for each 1 C of charge passing through the battery.

Potential difference (or voltage) is a measure of the difference in energy (per unit charge) across two points in a circuit.

TOP TIP

Voltage is measured in volts with a voltmeter.

Quick Test 5

1. What does charge experience in an electric field?
2. What do charges gain from a cell?
3. What units do we use to measure:

    (a) charge   (c) energy

    (b) current   (d) voltage?
4. What can the voltage across a component also be called?
5. The voltage on a battery is a measure of the energy given to the charges. True or false?
6. What is the symbol for a fuse?

d.c. and a.c.

Physics to learn	How to describe differences in alternating and direct current.
Success guide	You can give examples of d.c. and a.c. sources and distinguish d.c. and a.c. traces.

Electrical supply

There are two types of power supply: direct current (d.c.) and alternating current (a.c.).

d.c.
direct current

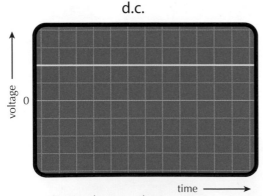

cell

battery

power supply

a.c.
alternating current

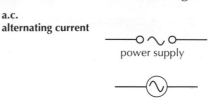

power supply

signal generator

Direct current flows in one direction around a circuit.

Examples of direct current: anything that uses battery power is using d.c.

A cathode ray oscilloscope (CRO) shows what the voltage across a steady d.c. supply looks like:

Alternating current repeatedly changes direction around a circuit.

Examples of alternating current: anything that uses mains power is using a.c.

A cathode ray oscilloscope (CRO) shows what the voltage across an a.c. supply looks like:

d.c.

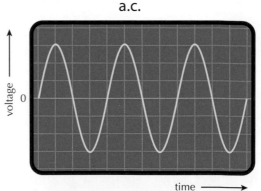

direct voltage => direct current

a.c.

alternating voltage => alternating current

> **TOP TIP**
> The CRO measures voltage on the y-axis and time on the x-axis.

Mains voltage

The frequency of the mains is 50 Hz. There are 50 complete waves every second. The flow of electrons increases and decreases, then increases and decreases in the opposite direction, 50 times every second. (Each complete cycle lasts $\frac{1}{50}$ s.)

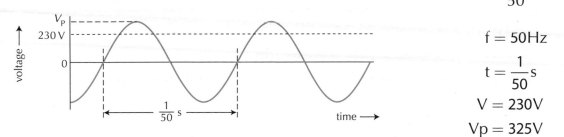

$$f = 50\text{Hz}$$
$$t = \frac{1}{50}\,\text{s}$$
$$V = 230\text{V}$$
$$Vp = 325\text{V}$$

For d.c., voltage and current are in one direction.

For a.c., the direction of voltage and current repeatedly reverses. The volume of voltage and current varies between zero and a peak value. Peak value is always greater than the rated or quoted value. The quoted value is the effective value.

Quick Test 6

1. What is the frequency of the Scottish mains supply?

2. If a battery is reversed, what happens to its signal on the CRO?

Components and symbols

Physics to learn	Practical circuit components and symbols.
Success guide	Describe the function and application of electrical and electronic symbols.

Symbols

An electrical component is a part of a circuit. Circuit symbols are used when we draw electrical components in a circuit diagram.

Component	Symbol	Description
Cell		• A source of voltage and energy. • Used to provide a steady d.c. supply in low power devices, such as remote controls.
Battery		• A series of cells. • Increased power from a series of cells. • Batteries can be small or the size of a room. • Alessandro Volta invented the first battery.
Bulb		• Converts electrical energy to light energy. • Used as a light in an electrical circuit or an output device in electronic circuits.
Switch		• **Closed:** Makes a circuit, current exists, ideally it has no resistance when closed. • **Open:** Breaks a circuit, no current, ideally it has infinite resistance when open.
Resistor		• A component that opposes current in a circuit. • The resistor converts electrical energy to heat energy. • Many components also have resistance.
Variable resistor		• A resistor whose resistance can be varied to change current. • Variable resistors can be used as volume controls or dimmer switches.
Voltmeter		• Measures voltage or potential difference in volts. • Connect in parallel.
Ammeter		• Measures electrical current in amperes. • Connect in series.

LED		• A light-emitting diode is often used as a low power output device to indicate on or off. • Recent developments mean we now have efficient LED lamps in the home.
Motor		• Converts electrical energy to kinetic energy. • Inside the motor electric current passes through a magnetic field to produce motion. • Motors are in everything from printers to washing machines.
Loudspeaker		• Converts electrical energy to sound energy. • Often used as the output device after an amplifier.
Photovoltaic cell		• Also called a solar cell, it is an electrical device that converts the energy of light directly into electricity by the photovoltaic effect. • Solar cells can power satellites, offshore buoys and be a domestic source of energy.
Fuse		• A wire in the fuse melts when the current goes too high. • Protects the wiring from overheating. • It is important to match the fuse size to the power of the appliance in use.
Diode		• Only allows current in one direction. • Can protect a circuit from a power supply being connected the wrong way or change a.c. power to d.c.
Capacitor		• Stores charge and energy. • Used in audio electronics to provide energy for peaks in demand, for time delay circuits and for camera flashes, among many uses.
Thermistor		• A resistor whose resistance can be changed with temperature. • Makes a good temperature sensor as an input device in electronics.
LDR		• A resistor whose resistance can be changed with light. • Makes a good light sensor as an input device in electronics.

Quick Test 7

1. What is the symbol for an LED?
2. Find a device that could be an input sensor.
3. Find a device that could be an output sensor.
4. Draw symbols for components from memory.

Series circuits

Physics to learn	Creating and measuring series circuits.
Success guide	Calculating current, voltages and resistances in series.

Series circuits

Series circuits have all the components in one loop.

There are no branches.

A series circuit is turned on or off by a single switch anywhere in the circuit.
A break in the circuit at any point causes the whole circuit to stop working.

Calculating current

The current is the same at all points round a series circuit.

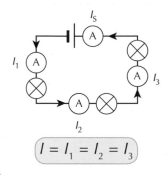

$$I = I_1 = I_2 = I_3$$

Charges flow round all points in the circuit at the same time.

Note how the ammeter is moved round the circuit to measure the current. It is always in line or in series in the circuit.

The ammeter readings will be the same all the way round.

Different circuits will have different readings but the values will still be the same all the way round.

Calculating voltage

The sum of the voltages across all the components in series is equal to the supply voltage.

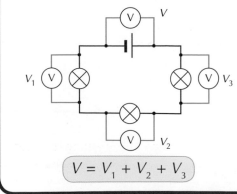

$$V = V_1 + V_2 + V_3$$

Note how the voltmeter is always placed across or in parallel with the component whose voltage is being measured.

The energy from the supply is shared out across the different components in the series circuit so each component gets a share of the voltage.

Each component will have a different voltage unless the components are identical.

Measuring resistance

Resistance is the opposition to current and is measured in ohms (Ω).

The total resistance in series is equal to the sum of the individual resistances.

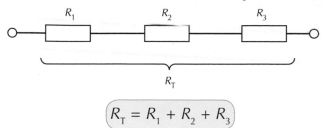

$$R_T = R_1 + R_2 + R_3$$

If we join components in series, we increase the resistance of the circuit. The current will decrease.

Potential dividers

Potential divider circuits use two or more resistors in series or a potentiometer to provide a part of a supply voltage (V_s).

The voltage divides in the ratio of the resistors:

$$\frac{V_1}{V_2} = \frac{R_1}{R_2}$$

$$V_2 = \frac{R_2}{R_T} \times V_s \quad \text{or} \quad V_2 = \frac{R_2}{R_1 + R_2} \times V_s$$

$R_T = R_{Total}$ and $V_s = V_{supply}$

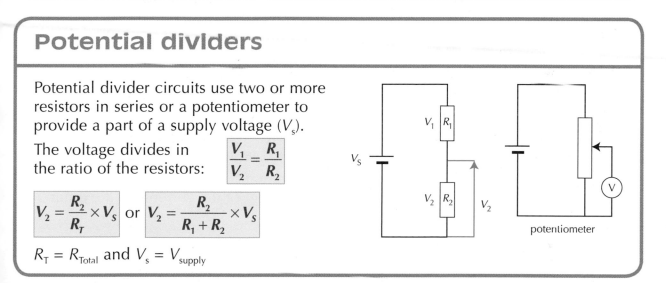

potentiometer

Quick Test 8

1. How are components connected in a series circuit?

2. 5, 10 and 15 ohm resistors are connected in series.

   (a) Calculate what voltage each gets from a 15 V supply.

   (b) If the current at the 10 ohm resistor is 0.5 A, calculate the current at the other resistors.

   (c) Calculate the total resistance of these resistors in series.

3. A 6 V battery is placed across three identical lamps in series. Calculate the voltage across the middle lamp.

Parallel circuits

Physics to learn	Creating and measuring parallel circuits.
Success guide	Calculating current, voltages and resistances in parallel.

Parallel circuits

Parallel circuits have branches and junctions. There is more than one path for the charges to follow. A break in one branch has no effect on the other branches. There can be a switch for, and in, each branch and there can be a master switch beside the supply for the whole circuit.

Calculating current

The circuit has different paths for charges to follow. **The current drawn from the supply depends on and is equal to the sum of the currents in the parallel branches.**

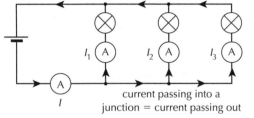

circuit has branches and more than one path to follow

current passing into a junction = current passing out

Note that I increases as more branches are added in parallel.

Each branch has its own current, independent of the currents in the other branches.

$$I = I_1 + I_2 + I_3$$

Calculating voltage

The voltages across components in parallel are the same and equal to their supply voltage.

$$V = V_1 = V_2 = V_3$$

The components can all be different yet they will all receive the same voltage as the supply voltage.

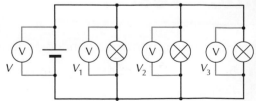

Conservation of energy

The energy supplied by the battery to each unit or coulomb of charge is equal to the energy given out by each unit or coulomb of charge. This is true for series or parallel circuits.

Calculating resistance

If we join components in parallel we decrease the resistance of the circuit. The current will increase.

The greater the number of branches, the smaller the total resistance and the greater the total current.

The total resistance of a parallel combination is calculated using a more complex formula.

$$\frac{1}{R_T} = \frac{1}{R_1} + \frac{1}{R_2} + \frac{1}{R_3}$$

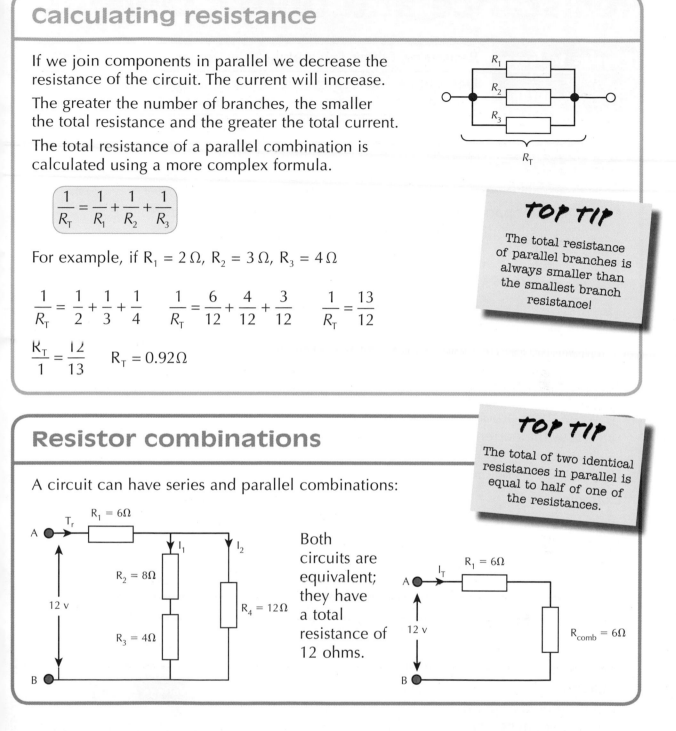

For example, if $R_1 = 2\,\Omega$, $R_2 = 3\,\Omega$, $R_3 = 4\,\Omega$

$$\frac{1}{R_T} = \frac{1}{2} + \frac{1}{3} + \frac{1}{4} \qquad \frac{1}{R_T} = \frac{6}{12} + \frac{4}{12} + \frac{3}{12} \qquad \frac{1}{R_T} = \frac{13}{12}$$

$$\frac{R_T}{1} = \frac{12}{13} \qquad R_T = 0.92\,\Omega$$

> **TOP TIP**
>
> The total resistance of parallel branches is always smaller than the smallest branch resistance!

Resistor combinations

> **TOP TIP**
>
> The total of two identical resistances in parallel is equal to half of one of the resistances.

A circuit can have series and parallel combinations:

Both circuits are equivalent; they have a total resistance of 12 ohms.

Quick Test 9

1. 5, 10 and 20 ohm resistors are connected in parallel. If the current at the 10 ohm resistor is 0.5 A, calculate the current at the other resistors. Calculate the total resistance of these three resistors in parallel.

2. A 6V battery is placed across a motor, a heater and a bulb all in parallel. Calculate the voltage across the heater.

Resistance and Ohm's law

Physics to learn	Resistance, Ohm's law and the effect of temperature.
Success guide	Describe resistance, investigate the relation between current, voltage and resistance, use graphs and calculate resistance.

Resistance

Materials can oppose the flow of charge through them. This is resistance.

with no resistors
in the circuit,
there will be a
large current

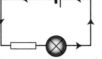

with a resistor in
the circuit,
there will be a
smaller current

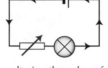

altering the value of
this variable resistor
changes the
brightness of the lamp

Resistance is measured in ohms (Ω) using an ohmmeter. 1Ω is the resistance between two points on a conductor when a constant potential difference of 1V between them produces a current of 1A. Increasing the resistance of a circuit decreases the current in that circuit.

Resistance can be calculated using: $\boxed{\textbf{Resistance} = \dfrac{\textbf{voltage}}{\textbf{current}}}$ $\boxed{R = \dfrac{V}{I}}$

Example

A current of 3 A is created in a circuit when a p.d. of 12V is applied across a motor.

Calculate the resistance of this motor. $R = \dfrac{V}{A} = \dfrac{12}{3} = 4\,\Omega.$

$$\triangle\ \frac{V}{I\ \ R}$$

Ohm's law

To further investigate the relationship between voltage and current across a fixed resistance, we can apply a range of voltages or potential differences across a resistor and measure the dependant currents.

Plotting the results of the experiment, the graph reveals a straight line passing through the origin.

Voltage (V)	Current (A)

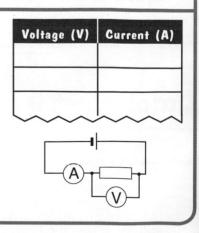

The shape of the graph shows the current in a resistor is directly proportional to the voltage applied.

This conclusion is known as Ohm's law.

The ratio $\frac{V}{I}$ remains constant for different currents.

$$R = \frac{V}{I} \qquad V = IR$$

Example

What voltage is needed to have a current of 2A in a circuit, when its resistance is $5\,\Omega$?

$V = IR = 2 \times 5 = 10\text{V}$

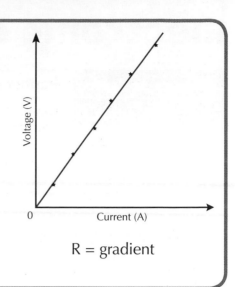

R = gradient

Resistance and temperature

A pupil repeated the Ohm's law experiment on two different torch bulbs.

The two bulbs show different gradients as they have different resistances.

However, while the current rises as the voltage increases, the current does not rise as much as expected. Why not?

As the voltage increases, the current increases and the bulb filament increases in temperature. This, in turn, increases the resistance of the filament instead of remaining constant. The current no longer increases in proportion.

TOP TIP

Ohm's law is one of the most important equations in electric circuits, $V = IR$.

Quick Test 10

1. When resistance decreases, what does current do?

2. What meter can measure resistance?

3. Calculate the voltage required to create a current of 1A in a $3\,\Omega$ resistor.

4. What assumption is made during the Ohm's law experiment?

5. A circuit resistance of $24\,\Omega$ is changed to $12\,\Omega$. What will happen to the current?

6. A variable resistor has its resistance changed from $10\,\Omega$ to $100\,\Omega$ while supplied by a voltage of 25V. Calculate the minimum and maximum current.

7. Calculate the current drawn from the mains voltage of 230V by a component of resistance $1\,\text{k}\Omega$. Calculate the current drawn if the component is used abroad with a voltage of 115V.

Electronic circuits

Physics to learn	Transistor circuits.
Success guide	You can identify and use the transistor.

Analogue and digital

Analogue signals are **continuously variable**. Most physical quantities, such as sound, heat and light, are analogue.

A microphone attached to an oscilloscope will display an analogue pattern with speech.

Digital signals have only two states. These are often called: **on/off, 5V/0V, high/low,** or **1/0**.

A CD player would output a digital pattern on an oscilloscope.

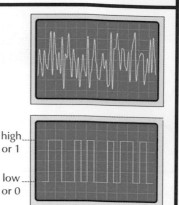

high
or 1

low
or 0

Input and output devices

Input	Output
Microphone Sound energy → electrical energy	**Loudspeaker** Electrical energy → sound energy
Solar cell Light energy → electrical energy	**Electric motor** Electrical energy → kinetic energy
Thermistor As temperature increases, its resistance decreases to ohmmeter	**Relay** Electrical energy → kinetic energy
Light dependent resistor (LDR) As light intensity increases, its resistance decreases to ohmmeter	**Light emitting diode (LED)** Electrical energy → light energy

Electronic circuits are made with INPUT → PROCESS → OUTPUT sub-systems.

The transistor will be our process sub-system.

TOP TIP

Note, the transistor has three connections.

The transistor

A transistor is an electronic switch. It is a voltage-controlled switch that responds to a change at the input.

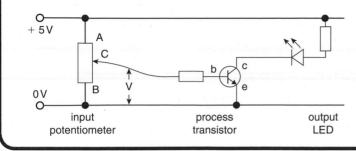

input
potentiometer

process
transistor

output
LED

When input $V > 0.7V$ then the transistor conducts and the LED has been switched on.

When input $V < 0.7V$ or negative then the transistor does not conduct and the LED goes off.

Transistor circuits

TOP TIP

Remember the transistor symbol.

Light-controlled circuits

As the light increases, the resistance of the LDR decreases, the input voltage decreases below 0.7V and the transistor does not conduct so the LED goes off. If light decreases, the LED goes on.

A light increase could switch on a security warning light.

A light decrease could switch on a night light.

The variable resistor is adjusted to set the light level for the transistor switching on or off.

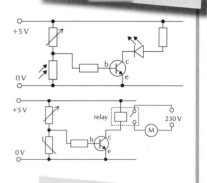

Temperature-controlled circuits

As temperature increases, the resistance of the LDR decreases, the input voltage decreases below 0.7V and the transistor does not conduct so the relay and motor go off. If temperature decreases, the relay and motor go on.

A temperature increase could switch on a fan.

A temperature decrease could switch on a heater.

TOP TIP

The MOSFET is another type of transistor

gate

drain

source

Quick Test 11

1. Describe an analogue signal.
2. Describe a digital signal.
3. What is the main purpose of a transistor in electronics?
4. Why is a LDR in series with a resistor at the input stage?
5. What is the purpose of the variable resistor?

Energy and power

Physics to learn	Energy and power. Estimate power ratings and energy consumption.
Success guide	Use the relationship between energy and power.

Energy

Around the house, circuits convert electrical energy into heat, light, kinetic, sound and potential energy.

Energy has the symbol E and is measured in joules (J).

Remember:

Kilojoule (kJ) = 1000 J (10_3 J)

Megajoule (MJ) = 1 000 000 J (10^6 J)

Gigajoule (GJ) = 1 000 000 000 J (10^9 J)

Terajoule (TJ) = 1 000 000 000 000 J (10^{12} J)

Power

Power (P) is measured in watts (W).

We can usually group the power of an appliance by the type of energy it produces. Appliances that transfer electrical energy to heat tend to be high power, whereas appliances that produce light from the electricity tend to be low power.

Appliance	Power rating
Cooker	12000 W
Kettle	2000 W
Iron	1900 W
Computer	250 W
TV	100 W
Radio	20 W
Light bulb	10 W
Clock	10 W

TOP TIP

Check the power of appliances in your home.

Energy, power and time

Power is the energy transferred or dissipated in unit time. The basic unit of time (t) in physics is the second (s).

A modern light bulb may have a power rating of 11 W. The light bulb converts 11 J of energy into light and a little heat every second.

$$\text{Power} = \frac{\text{Energy}}{\text{time}} \quad \boxed{P = \frac{E}{t}}$$

Energy can be measured directly with a joulemeter.

Time can be measured with a stop-clock.

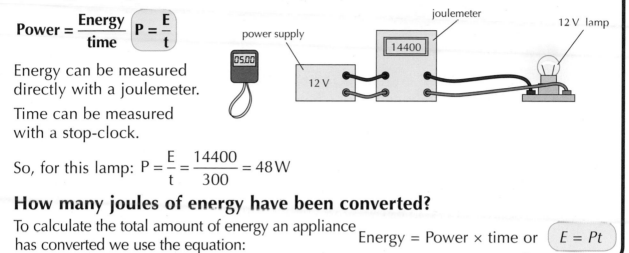

So, for this lamp: $P = \dfrac{E}{t} = \dfrac{14400}{300} = 48\,\text{W}$

How many joules of energy have been converted?

To calculate the total amount of energy an appliance has converted we use the equation:

Energy = Power × time or $\boxed{E = Pt}$

Energy consumption and energy meters

The joule is a very small unit of energy and electrical bills measure energy used in 'units'. To calculate units, power is left in kilowatts and time is kept in hours. 1 kW for 1 hour gives 1 unit of energy. A unit is 1 kilowatt hour.

Example

Calculate the energy used when a 2 kW fire is turned on for 6 hours. The cost of each unit is 15p.

$E = Pt = 2 \times 6 = 12\,\text{kWh}$ or 12 units.

Cost: $12 \times 15 = 180\text{p} = £1.80$

TOP TIP

$1\,\text{W} = 1\,\text{Js}^{-1}$

Quick Test 12

1. Name **three** high power appliances.
2. Calculate how much energy a 3 kW fire uses in 6 hours in joules.
3. An LED emits 1.2 J of light in 1 minute. What is its power rating?
4. How many joules of energy are there in 1 kilowatt-hour?
5. At a cost of 15p per unit, calculate the cost of:

    (a) a 14 W bulb on for 10 hours.

    (b) a 3000 W fire turned on for 5 hours.

    (c) a 2000 W tumble dryer used for 1 h 30 mins.

Electrical power

Physics to learn	Power equations, power transmission and power loss.
Success guide	Use appropriate relationship in electrical circuits.

Power equations

Power (P) is the energy (E) transferred in unit time (t) and is measured in watts (W).

As power rating increases, current increases. Power also depends on voltage. If the voltage supplied to a component in a circuit, e.g. a lamp, is decreased, the lamp will dim as it is now working at a lower power. In fact, the power rating can be confirmed to be equal to the product of voltage and current.

Power = current × voltage $\boxed{P = IV}$

If a voltage of 1V across a component creates a current of 1A, then the power is 1W, and 1J of energy will be transferred in a time of 1s.

More electrical power equations

If we substitute Ohm's law into our new power equation we can derive more:

Substituting $V = IR$ into $P = IV$, $\boxed{P = IV = I(IR) = I^2R}$

Substituting $I = \dfrac{V}{R}$ into $P = IV$, $\boxed{P = IV = \left(\dfrac{V}{R}\right)V = \dfrac{V^2}{R}}$

> **TOP TIP**
>
> We now have four equations we can use with electrical power:
>
> $P = \dfrac{E}{t}$
>
> $P = IV$
>
> $P = I^2R$
>
> $P = \dfrac{V^2}{R}$

Transmission of power

Electrical energy is carried in long transmission lines between the power station and our homes or industries. These lines make up part of the National Grid.

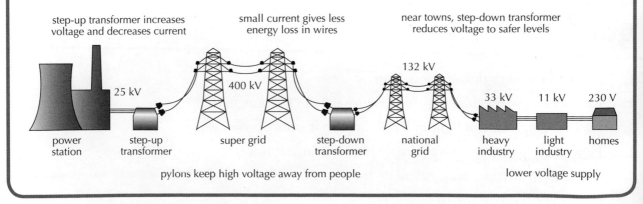

step-up transformer increases voltage and decreases current

small current gives less energy loss in wires

near towns, step-down transformer reduces voltage to safer levels

132 kV

25 kV · 400 kV · 33 kV · 11 kV · 230 V

power station · step-up transformer · super grid · step-down transformer · national grid · heavy industry · light industry · homes

pylons keep high voltage away from people

lower voltage supply

Power loss

Long transmission lines are made of low resistance cable, however, there is power loss in the lines and electrical energy will change to heat. For example, power is sent down transmission lines at the generated voltage of 25 kV, and 100 A of current is drawn through lines of resistance of 6 Ω.

The power sent, $P = IV = 100 \times 25\,000 = 2\,500\,000\,W$ or 2.5 MW.

$$\boxed{P_{loss} = I^2 R}$$

The power loss depends on the square of the current.

$P = I^2R = 100^2 \times 6 = 60\,000\,W$ or 60 kW

Plugs and fuses

Fuses are fitted to plugs to protect the flex, which can overheat if too large a current is drawn. The fuse may protect the appliance.

We know that mains voltage is 230 V. We check the power rating of an appliance then calculate what current will exist, e.g. for a heater rated at 2 kW:

$$I = \frac{P}{V} = \frac{2000}{230} = 8.7A$$

A fuse higher than the calculated current should be chosen. A 13A fuse should be used.

Quick Test 13

1. A drill uses 90 000 J of energy in 3 minutes. Calculate its power.

2. A 1.4 kW vacuum cleaner is used for 30 minutes. Calculate the energy it used.

3. A 3 V bulb draws 250 mA from a battery. What is its power? Calculate the energy used in 5 minutes.

4. A heater draws a current of 6 A through its 40 Ω element. Calculate its power rating.

5. Calculate the resistance of the filament of a 60 W, 230 V lamp.

6. Show that $P = IV$, $P = I^2R$ and $P = \dfrac{V^2}{R}$ are equivalent.

Heat

Physics to learn	Heat, temperature, kinetic theory and storing energy.
Success guide	Distinguish between heat and temperature. Use of materials in storing energy.

Heat and temperature

Temperature

Temperature (T) is a measure of how hot a substance is and it is measured in degrees Celsius (°C).

Some typical temperatures	
Absolute zero	−273°C
North Pole	−60°C
Melting ice	0°C
Room temperature	20°C
Core body temperature	37°C
Hot tap water	50°C
Boiling water	100°C
Sun	10^6°C

TOP TIP

Another unit used in physics for measuring temperature is the Kelvin scale. Where Celcius takes the freezing point of water as 0° the Kelvin scale takes the lowest possible temperature – absolute zero – as 0 (-273°C).

Heat

Heat, E_h, is a form of energy and is measured in joules (J).

Heat energy can transfer by conduction, convection or radiation.

Heat will flow from hot objects to colder surroundings. The greater the temperature difference with the surroundings, the greater the rate of heat loss.

Heat from an electrical heater can be measured directly with a joulemeter or can be calculated from the power of the heater and the time during which heat was provided using the equation:

$$E_h = P \times t$$

Heat can change temperature or can change the state of a material.

TOP TIP

Temperature => hotness, heat => energy.

Kinetic theory

Atoms or molecules are in constant motion. The movement of these particles depends on the amount of energy they have. This kinetic theory can be used to explain concepts such as pressure and temperature.

When a heater supplies energy to a liquid, the kinetic energy of the particles will increase and these particles will move about faster.

The temperature varies with the average kinetic energy of these atoms or molecules.

Storing energy

When heat energy is added to a material, it is stored in the material.

This effect is used in storage heaters, which store heat in an insulated container of hot water or bricks, using cheap electricity during off-peak times. These materials store a lot of heat and this stored heat can then be gradually released into a home during the day.

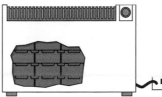

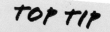

TOP TIP

Investigate new heating systems such as heat pumps and ground storage systems.

Quick Test 14

1. What quantity does temperature measure?
2. What quantity does heat measure?
3. Name **three** methods of heat transfer.
4. What is studied in kinetic theory?
5. What is stored when a material is heated?

Specific heat capacity

Physics to learn	Heat capacity and specific heat capacity.
Success guide	Can investigate relationships with heat, can measure and do calculations with specific heat capacity.

Heat capacity

Heat capacity is the amount of heat energy required to raise the temperature of a substance. It depends on three quantities: temperature change, the mass of the substance and the substance's material.

The greater the temperature change desired, the more energy will be required.

A greater mass of material will require a greater amount of heat for the same temperature rise.

Different materials require different quantities of energy to raise their temperature by one degree.

Temperature change

The quantity of heat energy required to raise the temperature of a substance varies with the change in temperature required ($E \alpha \Delta T$).

Mass Change

The quantity of heat energy required to raise the temperature of a substance varies with the mass of the subsitance.

Specific heat capacity

Specific heat capacity (c) is the quantity of energy required to change the temperature of 1 kg of mass of a substance by one degree Celsius.

This is also the energy 1 kg of a substance can store for each degree.

Water has a very high specific heat capacity:
$c = 4180 \, J \, kg^{-1} \, °C^{-1}$.

A lot of heat is needed to make water hot. Water can store a lot of heat.

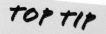

TOP TIP

The same quantity of energy used to heat up a substance will be given out when the substance cools.

TOP TIP

'varies with' = 'is directly proportional to'

Material change

The quantity of heat energy required to raise the temperature of a substance varies with the specific heat capacity of the material ($E \propto c$).

Energy (J) $\propto$ specific heat capacity ($J\,kg^{-1}\,°C^{-1}$).

Combining experiments shows heat energy depends on all three quantities:

$$E = cm\Delta T \qquad c = \frac{E}{m\Delta T} \qquad m = \frac{E}{c\Delta T} \qquad \Delta T = \frac{E}{cm}$$

Example

The energy required to raise the temperature of 3 kg of water from 20°C to 50°C is:

$$E = cm\Delta T = 4180 \times 3 \times 30 = 376\,200\,J.$$

Measuring specific heat capacity

This block of steel has holes drilled to take the heater and the thermometer. Oil conducts the heat. To measure the specific heat capacity:

- measure the **energy** supplied
- measure the mass of the block and the **temperature** rise
- then **calculate** using $c = \dfrac{E}{m\Delta T}$

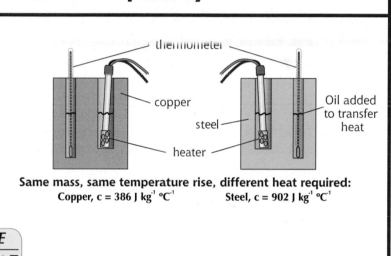

Same mass, same temperature rise, different heat required:
Copper, $c = 386\,J\,kg^{-1}\,°C^{-1}$ Steel, $c = 902\,J\,kg^{-1}\,°C^{-1}$

Quick Test 15

1. If you heat 1 kg of water in a kettle from room temperature of 20°C to boiling point of 100°C, how much energy does this take?

2. Calculate how long this kettle would take to boil if its power is 2200 W.

3. In practice, this kettle took 3 minutes. Why?

4. What is the unit of specific heat capacity?

5. A kettle gives out 167 200 J of heat energy when water at 100°C cools to 20°C. Calculate how much water is in the kettle.

Pressure

Physics to learn	Pressure, force and area.
Success guide	Explain pressure on a surface, calculate and measure pressure.

Pressure

Pressure is a measure of force on unit area. The combination of a large force on a small area exerts high pressure and is most likely to penetrate a surface. A small force on a large area exerts low pressure.

Examples of high pressure

Examples of low pressure

Pressure and kinetic theory of gases

Air particles exert pressure. Air pressure is caused by the weight of air above exerting force on the air molecules at ground or sea level.

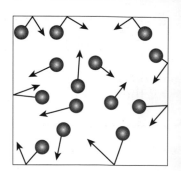

When we examine gas particles in a container we see that they are in constant motion. They have kinetic energy. They collide with each other but also against the walls of the container. Because of the motion, each molecule exerts a tiny force but all the particles exert a larger average force.

The force per unit area is the gas pressure.

Force is measured in newtons (N) and area in square metres (m^{-2}) so pressure can be measured in Nm^{-2}.

As more gas is pumped into the container, the number of moving particles increases, the number of particle collisions increases, the average force increases on the same area, and the pressure increases.

Calculating pressure

Pressure is the force per unit area, when the force is pushing on a surface.

$$\text{pressure} = \frac{\text{force}}{\text{area}} \qquad p = \frac{F}{A}$$

Units: Nm^{-2} or pascal (Pa). The pascal is a unit of pressure.

When 1 newton exerts a force on 1 square metre, the pressure is 1 pascal.

$1\ Pa = 1\ Nm^{-2}$

Example

A person whose mass is 80 kg stands on one foot. The foot has an area of $200\ cm^{-2}$. Calculate the pressure exerted on the floor.

$$200\ cm^{-2} = 2 \times 10^{-2}\ m^{-2} \qquad p = \frac{F}{A} = \frac{mg}{A} = \frac{80 \times 9.8}{2 \times 10^{-2}} = 3.9 \times 10^{4}\ Pa$$

Measuring pressure

Weights are added to the piston at the top of the syringe. The weights exert force on the area of piston in contact with the gas in the syringe.

The additional pressure exerted on the gas can be calculated from:

$p = \dfrac{F}{A} = \dfrac{mg}{A}$ where the contact area $A = \pi r^2$ and r is the radius of the piston which has been measured.

As the weights are added the change in pressure recorded by the sensor is seen to increase and the pressure values are shown to be equal to the calculated values of $\dfrac{F}{A}$, confirming the relationship.

> **TOP TIP**
> Atmospheric pressure is 101 000 Pa at sea or ground level.

Quick Test 16

1. A box is stood on end so that its contact area has been halved. What has happened to the weight and pressure on the floor?

2. Using kinetic theory, explain how pressure arises in a gas.

3. A box has a weight of 250 N and a contact area of $0.05\ m^{-2}$. Calculate the pressure on the floor.

4. An elephant has a mass of 7500 kg and stands on all four feet. If each foot has an area of $1000\ cm^{-2}$, what pressure is exerted?

5. If the same elephant stood on one foot, what would be its pressure?

Heating a gas

Physics to learn	Pressure law, Charles' law, kinetic theory.
Success guide	Explain the effect of changing temperature on pressure or volume. Derive and use the Kelvin temperature scale.

Pressure law

Fixed volume and mass of air is trapped in a flask, and the flask is placed in water.

The water is heated and stirred.

The temperature in °C is measured with a thermometer or temperature sensor. The pressure in Pa or kPa is measured with a bourdon gauge or pressure sensor.

As the temperature rises, the pressure rises. There is a linear relationship between the temperature and the pressure. However, at 0°C there is still pressure as the line of best fit does not go through the origin.

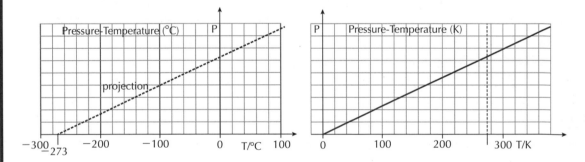

Only if we extend the line back to where there is zero pressure will there be a true zero of temperature. From the experiment, zero pressure is predicted at –273°C. Zero pressure indicates the true zero of temperature, called absolute zero. We need to change from the Celsius scale to the Kelvin scale.

Absolute zero is 0 K. The Kelvin scale uses the same division size as the Celsius scale.

On the Kelvin scale, pressure is directly proportional to temperature: p α T.

TOP TIP

Only with temperature in Kelvin will this gas law work!

$$\boxed{\frac{p}{T} = k}$$ where k is a constant. $\boxed{\dfrac{p_1}{T_1} = \dfrac{p_2}{T_2}}$

This is known as the pressure law.

Example

A sealed flask of gas has a pressure of 5×10^5 Pa at a temperature of 27°C. If the temperature drops to –27°C, what is the new pressure?

$p_1 = 5 \times 10^5$ Pa

$T_1 = 27°C = 300\,K$

$T_2 = -27°C = 246\,K$

$$\frac{P_1}{T_1} = \frac{P_2}{T_2} \qquad \frac{5 \times 10^5}{300} = \frac{P_2}{246} \qquad p_2 = 4.1 \times 10^5\,Pa$$

Kinetic theory: the pressure law

If the temperature increases, the particles have more kinetic energy and the velocity increases. The particles hit the container walls more often and with greater force. Area (A) remains constant but average force (F) increases so the pressure (p) increases: $p = \dfrac{F}{A}$.

Charles' law

Air is trapped in a thin glass rod by a bead of mercury. As the bead is free to move, the pressure of the gas will always be the same as the pressure of the atmosphere. We say that during the experiment there is a gas with a fixed mass and a constant pressure.

The experiment considers the relationship between volume and temperature. The water is heated and stirred. The temperature must rise slowly so that the gas is evenly heated and is the same temperature as the water.

The temperature in °C is measured with a thermometer or temperature sensor. The volume is measured with a scale on the rule behind the rod.

As the temperature rises the volume rises also. There is a linear relationship between the temperature and the volume.

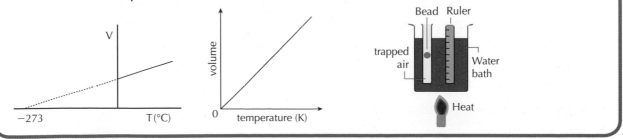

On the Kelvin scale, volume is directly proportional to temperature:

$$V \alpha T \qquad \boxed{\frac{V}{T} = k} \qquad \boxed{\frac{V_1}{T_1} = \frac{V_2}{T_2}}$$

TOP TIP
Remember temperatures in Kelvins.

This is **Charles' law**.

Example

At what temperature will a litre of trapped gas be doubled in volume if it started at 0°C?

$$0°C = 273 \, K. \quad \frac{V_1}{T_1} = \frac{V_2}{T_2} \quad \frac{1}{273} = \frac{2}{T_2} \quad T_2 = 546K$$

New temperature = 546 K or 273°C.

Kinetic theory: Charles' law

If the temperature increases, the particles have more kinetic energy and the velocity increases. The particles hit the container walls with more force. The volume increases so the surface area increases to keep the pressure constant.

The pressure, p, is constant: $p = \dfrac{F}{A}$. F increases and A increases.

Temperatures

What is double the temperature of 20°C? We cannot just double 20!
First change to the Kelvin scale: 20°C = 293 K.
Now double, which makes 586K.
To return to Celsius, subtract 273.
This gives 313°C.

TOP TIP
A temperature change of 100°C = a temperature change of 100K. The divisions are the same size.

Temperature scales

Only the Kelvin scale starts from an absolute zero of temperature.

- Degrees Celsius to Kelvin: add 273.
- Kelvin to degrees Celsius: subtract 273.

Quick Test 17

1. Air at 5°C and 1.25×10^5 Pa is heated by the Sun to 25°C. Calculate the new pressure.
2. What assumptions did you make in Q1?
3. At 25°C, the volume of a fixed mass of gas is 3 litres. Calculate its volume at 125°C.

General gas theory

Physics to learn	Boyle's law, general gas equation, kinetic theory.
Success guide	Explain and calculate the effect of changing volume on pressure, with or without temperature change.

Boyle's law

A quantity of air, with a fixed mass and constant temperature, is trapped in a column.

Pressure is measured with a bourdon gauge or a pressure sensor connected to a computer. The volume is read from a scale on the column.

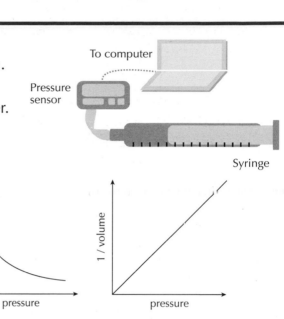

The space in the column is decreased, decreasing the volume. As this happens, the pressure increases.

Halving the volume doubles the pressure.

A graph of pressure against volume is not a straight line but indicates an inverse relationship.

The pressure is proportional to the inverse of volume.

$p \alpha \dfrac{1}{V}$ $pV = k$ where k is a constant $p_1 V_1 = p_2 V_2$. This

is Boyle's law.

Kinetic theory: Boyle's law

As the temperature is constant, the kinetic energy and the velocity are constant.

If the volume is increased, the particles hit the container walls less often, therefore they exert less average force on the increased area of the container walls.

The pressure (p) decreases as force F decreases and area A increases:

$$p = \frac{F}{A}$$

TOP TIP

$1 \times 10^6 \text{ cm}^3 = 1 \text{ m}^3$

TOP TIP

Various units can be used in Boyle's law if the same on both sides.

General gas equation

There are times when all three of the quantities – pressure, volume and temperature – all change together. The three gas laws that we have found from experiments can be combined into one general gas equation. P, V, and T can all change.

Experiment 1: **Pressure law** $\dfrac{p_1}{T_1} = \dfrac{p_2}{T_2}$ $\dfrac{P}{T}$ = a constant

Experiment 2: **Charles' law** $\dfrac{V_1}{T_1} = \dfrac{V_2}{T_2}$ $\dfrac{V}{T}$ = a constant

> **TOP TIP**
> The mass of gas must remain constant.

Experiment 3: **Boyle's law** $p_1V_1 = pV_2$ PV = a constant

Combining the equations gives:

$\dfrac{p_1V_1}{T_1} = \dfrac{p_2V_2}{T_2}$ $\dfrac{pV}{T}$ = a constant. This is the general gas equation.

> **TOP TIP**
> The temperature of gas must be in the Kelvin scale.

The general equation can be used in all gas calculations instead of the three individual equations.

A constant quantity will simply cancel, e.g. $T_1 = T_2 \Rightarrow$ equation 3. So the general gas equation is the most useful one to remember – it's four equations in one!

In the pressure law, mass and volume are constant.

In Charles' law, mass and pressure are constant.

In Boyle's law, mass and temperature are constant.

Quick Test 18

1. A deep-sea diver is down where the pressure is 3×10^5 Pa. He breathes out air bubbles of volume 2×10^{-6} m^3. What volume will they have at the surface where the pressure is 1×10^5 Pa?

2. A 3 litre gas cylinder at 0°C has a pressure of 6×10^5 Pa. If the gas is used where the temperature is 27°C and the pressure is 1×10^5 Pa, calculate:

   (a) the volume the gas will occupy

   (b) the volume available.

3. What must be kept constant for all the gas equations?

Waves

Physics to learn	Longitudinal and transverse waves.
Success guide	Describe waves, distinguish and give examples of longitudinal and transverse waves.

Energy waves

A wave is a movement of energy. Energy can be transferred from one place to another by a wave. In some waves, energy moves through materials but other waves are simply a movement of energy though space.

There are many types of waves including:

water waves, sound waves, light, heat, radio and other electromagnetic waves.

Energy moves across the ocean and the water moves up and down.

Sound energy travels through the air and the particles vibrate.

Radio waves can travel through space as well as through the air.

boat bobs up and down

loudspeaker vibrates

air particles vibrate

Longitudinal waves

Sound requires a medium or particles to travel through. Sound can pass through solids, liquids and gases but cannot pass through a vacuum. Sound is a **longitudinal** wave. The speaker cone below vibrates and the air particles vibrate in the same direction. The vibrations are in line with the direction of movement of energy.

loudspeaker   candle flame   air particles vibrate   energy moves along

Wiggling a slinky can show that energy moves along but the coils just vibrate. When the particles are compressed this is labelled **compression** and when the particles are spaced out this is known as **rarefaction**.

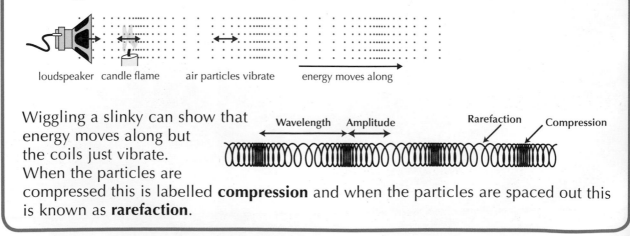

Wavelength   Amplitude   Rarefaction   Compression

The more energy that is put into a wave, the greater its **amplitude**, that is, the particles or molecules will vibrate more. Amplitude is measured in metres (m). Amplitude is the maximum distance a particle will be displaced from the normal position.

Transverse waves

Water waves and electromagnetic waves are all **transverse** waves. **Electromagnetic** waves include radio waves, microwaves, infrared radiation, visible light, ultraviolet radiation, X-rays and gamma rays.

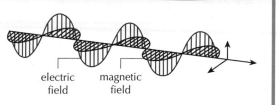

electric field   magnetic field

Water waves need the particles of water for the energy to travel through but electromagnetic waves are oscillations of electric and magnetic fields and so can travel through a vacuum.

The vibrations are at right angles to the direction of movement of energy. A wave can be sent along a rope to illustrate a transverse wave. The source moves up and down, the particles move up and down but the direction of energy movement is at right angles to this.

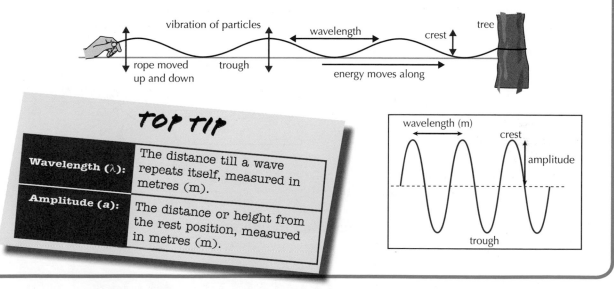

TOP TIP

Wavelength (λ):	The distance till a wave repeats itself, measured in metres (m).
Amplitude (a):	The distance or height from the rest position, measured in metres (m).

Quick Test 19

1. State what sound cannot travel through.
2. What is in a wave moving across the ocean?
3. What is the opposite of a compression?
4. How many waves are shown in the transverse rope above?
5. If the peak to trough height is 0.5 m, calculate the amplitude of the waves.
6. If a longitudinal slinky is 10 m long, calculate the wavelength.

Wave equations

Physics to learn	Wave measurements.
Success guide	Use relationships between wave speed, frequency, wavelength, distance and time.

Waves

The signal generator creates electrical signals.

The loudspeaker turns electrical energy into sound energy, which is heard as longitudinal waves.

The oscilloscope changes electrical energy into light energy, which is seen as a transverse wave.

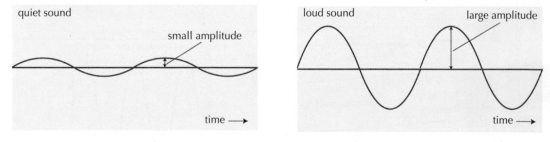

Adjust the **volume**: louder volume → **increased amplitude**.

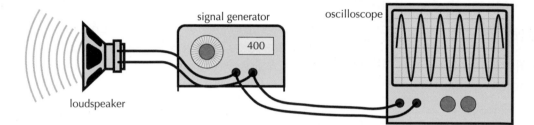

Adjust the **pitch**: higher pitch → **increased frequency**.

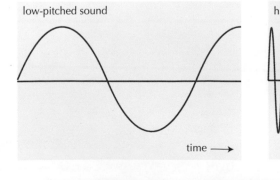
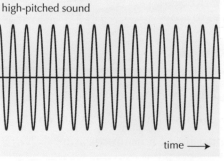

Period and frequency

The period (T) is the time to produce one wave and it is measured in seconds (s). If 10 waves take a time of 0.2 seconds, the time for one wave

is $\frac{0.2}{10} = 0.02\,\text{s}$.

The frequency (f) of a signal is the number of waves produced in the unit time, e.g. 1 second.

$$frequency = \frac{number}{time} \qquad \boxed{f = \frac{n}{t}}$$

Frequency is measured in hertz, e.g. if 10 waves pass a point in a time of 0.2 seconds,

the frequency, $f = \frac{n}{t}$ $f = \frac{10}{0.2}$ $f = 50\,\text{Hz}$.

If we know the time for one wave, the period, then the equation for frequency

becomes $\boxed{f = \frac{1}{T}}$.

Wavelength and frequency

Transverse water waves can be studied in a ripple tank.

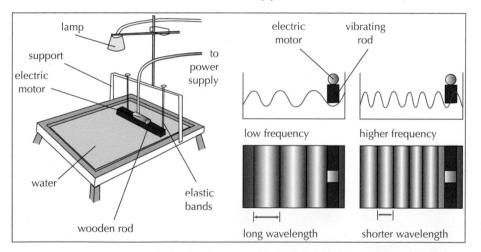

The frequency of the motor and rod is the same as the frequency of the water waves. Increase the frequency and the wavelength decreases.

The speed of the water waves does not change as the frequency and wavelength change, provided the waves move in the same depth of water.

$$speed = \frac{distance}{time} \qquad \boxed{v = \frac{d}{t}}$$

TOP TIP

When we study waves on the electromagnetic spectrum we find that as the frequency increases, the wavelength decreases.

Measuring wave speed

The speed (v) is the distance travelled in unit time. Speed is measured in metres/second (ms^{-1}).

We can measure the speed of sound in air in the lab.

- Measure a distance, say, 1 m.
- Place two microphones this distance apart attached to an electronic timer or computer and interface.
- The timer starts timing when the sharp sound of the hammer passes microphone 1 and stops timing when the sound passes microphone 2.
- Then calculate using $speed = \dfrac{distance}{time}$ $v = \dfrac{d}{t}$

The speed of sound is around 340 ms^{-1} in air. The time for sound to travel 1 m will be around 3 ms so the electronic timer will need to measure milliseconds or microseconds.

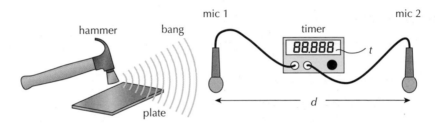

The speed of light is so fast that on Earth light appears to travel instantly. During thunder and lightning we do notice the large difference between the speed of sound and the speed of light.

The speed of light is accepted to be 3×10^8 ms^{-1} in a vacuum or in air. The speed of light is almost 1 million times faster than the speed of sound.

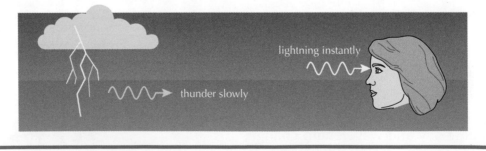

The wave equation

The speed of a wave is also related to its frequency and wavelength. If the distance travelled by a wave is one wavelength, the time taken is one period.

$$v = \frac{d}{t} \quad v = \frac{1\lambda}{1T} \quad \text{Now } f = \frac{1}{T}$$

so $v = f\lambda$ (the 'wave equation'.)

TOP TIP

The wavelengths of light are from 400 to 700 nanometers (nm).

TOP TIP

In a rearranged wave equation, v remains on the top.

For example: a wave has a frequency of 15 Hz and has a wavelength of 2 cm. Calculate its speed. Remember to change cm to m.

$$v = f\lambda = 15 \times 0.02 = 0.3 \text{ ms}^{-1}$$

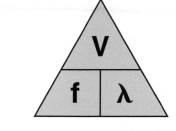

$v = f\lambda$ $\lambda = \dfrac{v}{f}$ $f = \dfrac{v}{\lambda}$

Wave measurement

Frequency (f): The number of waves in unit time.	hertz (Hz).
Period (T): The time for one wave (to pass).	seconds (s)
Velocity (v): The distance travelled in unit time.	metres/second (ms^{-1})
Velocity (v): The product of frequency and wavelength.	metres/second (ms^{-1})

Quick Test 20

1. A wave has a frequency of 10 Hz. What does this mean?
2. Thunder travels 1 km. Calculate approximately how long this takes.
3. There are 20 waves passing a point in 4 s. Calculate the:
   (a) frequency
   (b) period
4. Calculate the speed a wave of frequency 5000 Hz and length 0.02 m is travelling at.
5. What is the wavelength of sound of frequency 256 Hz (middle C) in air?

Diffraction

Physics to learn	Describe diffraction of waves.
Success guide	Explain the effect of wavelength on sound, water, radio and microwaves.

Diffraction

Waves can bend around an object or obstacles. For example, the line of sight is blocked but sound is still heard because of the sound spreading out from a doorway. The waves do not simply pass straight through but spread out after passing through the gap.

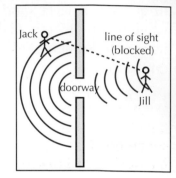

The bending, called **diffraction**, occurs at both edges or at gaps. We can think of a gap as being made of two edges. We can examine diffraction in a ripple tank.

Edges

As the waves pass the edge the energy spills to the side and the waves change from plane wavefronts to circular wavefronts.

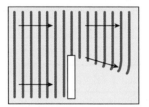
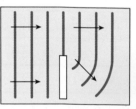

Long wave (LW), low frequency wavelengths diffract more than short wave (SW), high frequency wavelengths.

Gaps

A gap is created that is wider than the wavelength of the waves. Through the centre, the waves continue undisturbed. At each edge the waves show diffraction.

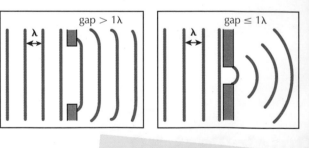

Circular wave-fronts are produced when the width of the gap is less than or equal to the size of the wavelength of the waves.

The wavelengths of sounds are about the same size as the width of doorways.

TOP TIP

If the wavelength decreases, the gap also needs to decrease to see diffraction.

Radio waves

Diffraction of radio

Radio waves have the longest wavelengths of the electromagnetic wave spectrum and range from about 100 kilometres to 1 millimetre.

The longest wavelengths will travel the furthest over hills because of their ability to diffract well.

Analogue TV waves are also radio waves but these have shorter wavelengths than radio station broadcast waves.

Digital satellite TV waves are also radio waves. These are known as microwaves as they occupy the shortest of the radio wavelengths.

Microwaves are used for satellite communication – they travel well in straight lines to and from the satellites in space because they exhibit little diffraction. Satellite receivers need line-of-sight views of the satellite in space.

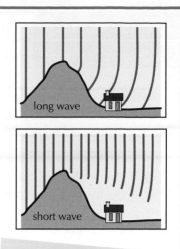

long wave

short wave

TOP TIP

Radio waves have a longer wavelength than TV waves. Radio waves diffract more than TV waves.

Calculating wavelength

To calculate the wavelength of a radio wave we can use the wave equation.

All radio waves travel at 3×10^8 ms^{-1} through the air or space.

Example

If the frequency of a radio wave is 2 GHz, what is its wavelength?

$$\lambda = \frac{v}{f} = \frac{3 \times 10^8}{2 \times 10^9} = 0.15 \text{m}$$

Quick Test 21

1. What is the meaning of diffraction?
2. What wavelengths bend most?
3. What are microwaves?
4. Why are radios still usable behind mountains?
5. Why does a satellite dish need to 'see' the satellite?

Electromagnetic spectrum: facts

Physics to learn	Bands of the electromagnetic spectrum.
Success guide	Relative frequency and wavelength. Sources and applications.

Bands of the spectrum

The electromagnetic spectrum is made up of a very wide range of wavelengths. All the waves are transverse. The waves are put into bands or regions depending on how they act on matter or how they are made.

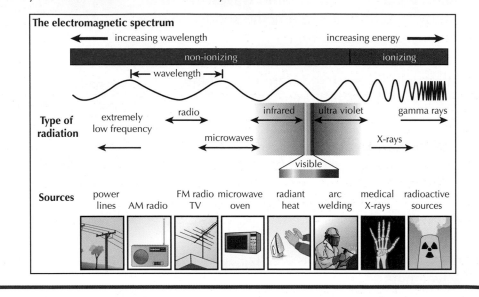

The electromagnetic spectrum

increasing wavelength   increasing energy

non-ionizing   ionizing

wavelength

Type of radiation: extremely low frequency — radio — microwaves — infrared — ultra violet — visible — X-rays — gamma rays

Sources: power lines — AM radio — FM radio TV — microwave oven — radiant heat — arc welding — medical X-rays — radioactive sources

Sources and applications

Gamma rays

Gamma rays can be emitted from natural materials (such as some rocks, e.g. granite) and from man-made materials (such as some materials found in power stations). A lot of gamma rays are produced in the Universe and are travelling through space. Gamma rays have very high frequency, very short wavelength and high energy. They can be detected with photographic film or with a geiger counter. They can be used in radioactive tracers or to kill cancer cells.

Instruments and syringes can be sterilised with gamma rays to kill bacteria. Gamma rays penetrate so well they can also be used to detect cracks in metals.

X-rays

X-rays have high frequency and high energy. X-rays are produced from X-ray tubes. Hot gases in the universe also emit X-rays. They can penetrate tissue and be detected on photographic film. Doctors and dentists use X-rays to examine our bones and teeth. Doctors can also look for ulcers in your guts – you swallow a barium meal, which absorbs X-rays, then ulcers can be detected by the X-rays. X-rays can treat some cancers.

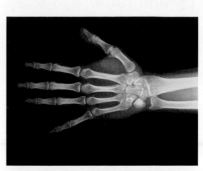

Ultraviolet

UV tubes and the Sun are sources of ultraviolet. They cause certain materials, often white, to fluoresce. Although the atmosphere stops many of these rays reaching us on Earth, they can cause suntans or give us skin cancer. Hidden marks on banknotes will fluoresce under a UV lamp. UV has a higher frequency and energy than visible light.

Visible light

Light is emitted from hot filaments of lamps, from stars and even fireflies. In physics, white is not a colour at all, but rather the combination of all the colours of the visible light spectrum. In 1672, when describing his discovery that light could be split into many colours by a prism, Isaac Newton gave the seven colours as red, orange, yellow, green, blue, indigo, violet. Violet has the shortest wavelength and red the longest.

Infrared

Infrared rays (heat waves) have a lower frequency than visible light rays. We think of infrared more as heat as it can be felt on our skin. Infrared rays are absorbed by our skin and we feel warm. Invisible heat rays are given out by all warm bodies. Thermograms are colour heat photos of this radiation. If an infrared camera takes your photo you will not notice it as the rays are invisible. Burglars beware!

Microwaves

Above radio we find microwaves with a higher frequency (in the GHz range). Microwaves diffract (bend) very little though, compared with radio waves. Microwaves are sent to and from satellites. Microwaves are used from space by astronomers to find out about the structure of galaxies. Microwaves are used with mobile phones and for cooking.

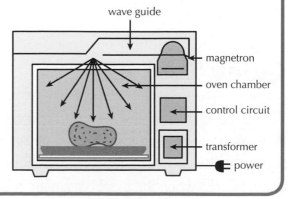

wave guide
magnetron
oven chamber
control circuit
transformer
power

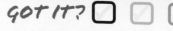
TV and radio

TV and radio waves have the longest wavelengths in the electromagnetic spectrum. They diffract round obstacles to get to our homes. Transmitters and receivers are used to send and detect these signals. Radio waves are also emitted by stars and gases in space and tell us more about matter in the Universe.

Researching the spectrum

We have learned that the electromagnetic spectrum contains bands with a wide range of different applications. This can be researched further, either individually or in a group. Create a project and compare with others your findings. Concentrate on sources, detectors, applications, limitations and safety concerns.

Compare the frequency and the wavelengths of the different parts of the spectrum.

TOP TIP

Learn the order by frequency and wavelength of the electromagnetic spectrum.

Quick Test 22

1. List the bands of the electromagnetic spectrum in order.
2. What bands have a shorter wavelength than light?
3. What bands have a longer wavelength than light?
4. Find out when the electromagnetic spectrum was created.
5. List sources of electromagnetic waves.
6. List applications of electromagnetic waves.

Electromagnetic spectrum: data

Physics to learn	Relationships: frequency and energy, frequency and wavelength.
Success guide	Velocity calculations with frequency and wavelength.

The spectrum

We have discovered that the electromagnetic spectrum has extremely long waves at one end of the spectrum and extremely short waves at the other end of the spectrum. In fact, useful radio waves may be kilometres long, yet at the other end useful gamma rays may have wavelengths less than the diameter of an atom.

Velocity

Most of the electromagnetic spectrum is invisible to our eyes. Only the colours of light are visible. It is known that charge has an electric field around it and that moving charges (such as in an electric current) give a magnetic field. In 1861, James Clark Maxwell made the connection between electricity, magnetism and the speed of light. He concluded that light was an electromagnetic wave.

Experimental measurements of the speed of light and electromagnetic waves can be made to a very high degree of certainty. More than this, by using knowledge of electricity and magnetism, physicists have calculated exactly what the speed of light and all electromagnetic waves should be: $299\ 792\ 458\ ms^{-1}$ in a vacuum.

Velocity through a vacuum or air

For all our calculations we will use the speed of light and all electromagnetic waves to three significant figures, i.e. 300 million ms^{-1}.

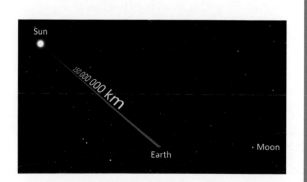

The speed of light and all electromagnetic waves is 300 000 000 ms^{-1}.

Using scientific notation:

$$v = 3 \times 10^8\ ms^{-1}$$

Air is mainly empty space, and even atoms are mostly empty space. So the speed of light through air is taken as the same as the speed of light through a vacuum: $v = 3 \times 10^8\ ms^{-1}$.

Velocity through dense materials

However, light does travel slower through optically dense materials. In normal glass, light travels at:

$$V_{\text{light in glass}} = 200\,000\,000\,\text{ms}^{-1} \quad \text{or} \quad V_{\text{light in glass}} = 2 \times 10^8\,\text{ms}^{-1}$$

In more optically dense materials, e.g. diamond, light travels even slower.

Many waves of the electromagnetic spectrum cannot travel through materials, but other waves of the spectrum can travel through material as if it is not there! Why not research this area?

Frequency and wavelength

As we move through the electromagnetic spectrum from radio waves to gamma rays, the wavelength decreases dramatically. At the same time, and as the velocity does not change, this means that frequency increases dramatically.

As frequency increases and wavelength decreases the product has been found to be a constant and equal to the velocity.

Frequency, wavelength and velocity are related by the wave equation:

velocity = frequency × wavelength

$$v = f\lambda$$

Alternatively: $f = \dfrac{v}{\lambda}$ $\qquad$ $\lambda = \dfrac{v}{f}$

Frequency is the number of waves per second and is measured in hertz.

Wavelength is the distance till the wave repeats, measured in metres.

Velocity is measured in metres per second.

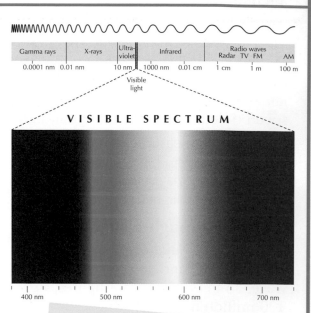

VISIBLE SPECTRUM

400 nm　　500 nm　　600 nm　　700 nm

TOP TIP

Two equations for wave speed:
$$v = \frac{d}{t} \text{ and } v = f\lambda.$$

Example

What is the frequency of red light with wavelength 650 nm?
(n = nano, 10^{-9})

$$f = \frac{v}{\lambda} = \frac{3 \times 10^8}{650 \times 10^{-9}} = 4.6 \times 10^{14}\,\text{Hz}$$

Frequency and energy

As frequency increases, the wave radiations have more energy. In fact, just over 100 years ago this relationship was first discovered and developed by two famous physicists, Max Planck and Albert Einstein. They considered the radiation of the electromagnetic spectrum to be made of small bundles of energy called photons. The higher the frequency each photon had, the more energy it had.

Gamma radiation has the most energy and can be very dangerous. X-rays can aid the diagnosis of disease and damage in our bodies but the number of images that can safely be taken is usually limited. Ultraviolet can give you a suntan but this is also a sign of damage. Some people think microwaves from mobile phones can damage children's brains: should they use them? Could you use your scientific knowledge to discuss this with the public?

Quick Test 23

1. What is the speed of radio waves in a vacuum?
2. What is the speed of X-rays through the air?
3. What is the speed of light through normal glass?
4. A gamma ray has a frequency of 1×10^{12} Hz. Calculate its wavelength.
5. A radio wave has a wavelength of 1 km. Calculate its frequency.
6. An electromagnetic wave has a length of 10^6 m. What part of the spectrum does it belong to?

Refraction of light

Physics to learn	Refraction of light. Optical terminology.
Success guide	Velocity, angles and applications.

Refraction and velocity

Refraction occurs when light moves from one optical density of material to another.

Glass is optically more dense than air. If light moves from air to glass, velocity decreases. Light travels at 3×10^8 ms^{-1} in air and about 2×10^8 ms^{-1} in glass.

If we could observe the wavefronts or the 'crests' of light we would notice that they behave in a similar manner to water waves when they cross a shallow region in a ripple tank. As velocity decreases, wavelength decreases and the ratio of $\frac{v}{\lambda}$ remains constant.

Frequency is constant, $\left(f = \dfrac{v_{air}}{\lambda_{air}} = \dfrac{v_{glass}}{\lambda_{glass}} \right)$

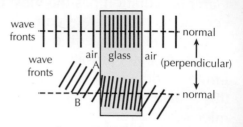

refraction through a parallel plate

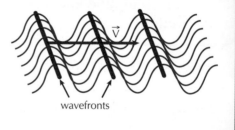

wavefronts

Refraction and direction

The change in velocity during refraction at an angle will produce a change in direction.

- **Air to glass:** When a ray of light enters a more dense medium it slows down and bends towards the normal.
- **Glass to air:** When a ray of light enters a less dense medium it speeds up and bends away from the normal.

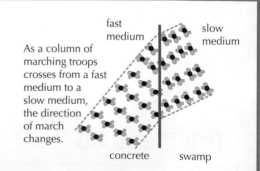

As a column of marching troops crosses from a fast medium to a slow medium, the direction of march changes.

The angle in the more dense medium is smaller than the angle in the less dense medium. This rule is independent of whether the ray is entering or emerging from the medium.

Applications of refraction

If we have an eye defect, refraction allows additional lenses to further change the direction of light rays, thus correcting eye defects.

A **convex** lens is a typical converging lens.

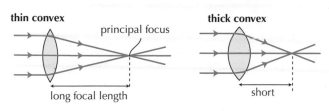

A **concave** lens is a typical diverging lens.

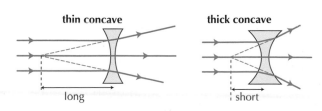

Reversibility of light

Light rays are reversible. A ray enters glass at 60°, it will refract to 35°. In reverse, the ray meeting the boundary at 35° leaves the glass at 60°.

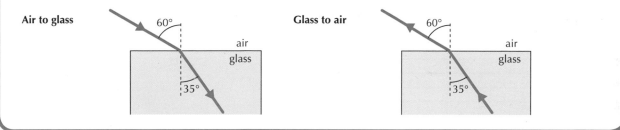

Quick Test 24

1. State what changes occur when light goes straight into a tank of water.
2. What happens to the frequency of waves during refraction?
3. What happens to the wavelength of waves during refraction?
4. What direction does light take going from glass to air at an angle?
5. Name a medical use for refraction.

Critical angle and TIR

Physics to learn	Limits of refraction, critical angle.
Success guide	Angles of refraction, simple applications.

Limits of refraction

A ray of light is directed into a glass prism. We know that when light enters a more optically dense material it refracts and the angle in the glass is smaller than the angle in the air.

The incident ray makes an angle of incidence, i, with the normal.

The refracted ray makes an angle of refraction, r, with the normal.

From air to glass: $r < i$

An experiment can be done to confirm this theory. As the angle of incidence increases, the angle of refraction increases also, but it is always smaller in the glass.

Angle of incidence, i (°)	Angle of refraction, r (°)
0	0
10	6.6
20	13.2
30	19.5
40	25.4
50	30.7
60	35.3
70	38.8
80	41.0
90	??

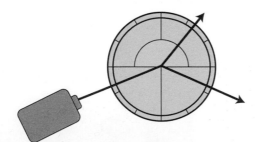

As the angle of incidence increases towards 90°, the angle of refraction is seen to reach a limit. In fact, if we try to illuminate the angles beyond this limit we find we cannot do so.

TOP TIP

The limit angle is what we know as the critical angle.

Critical angle

Light rays are reversible.

When light travelling through glass hits the inner surface of the glass the angle of incidence decides whether light will refract out or reflect in.

1. The angle of incidence is small. The ray passes from glass to air and refracts.
2. The angle of incidence is large. The ray is reflected. This is known as **total internal reflection** (TIR).

Refraction

The angle of incidence (i) is small, less than the critical angle C. The ray passes out of the glass and is refracted.

Critical angle

The angle of incidence (i) is now at the critical angle C. The angle of refraction is now 90°. The ray emerges along the glass block. Some of the light is also reflected.

Total internal reflection

The angle of incidence (i) is large, greater than the critical angle C. The ray is totally internally reflected. The angle of reflection is equal to the angle of incidence.

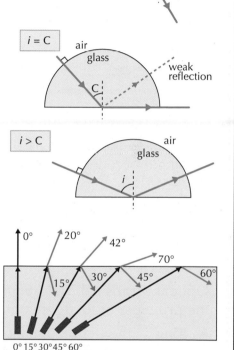

The critical angle for water is close to 49°, not the same as for glass.

Quick Test 25

1. State what is meant by the critical angle.
2. State what is meant by total internal reflection.
3. How do you measure the critical angle?

Total internal reflection and optical fibres

Physics to learn	Optical fibres and uses.
Success guide	Use refraction, critical angle and total internal reflection in applications.

Reflection from a plane mirror

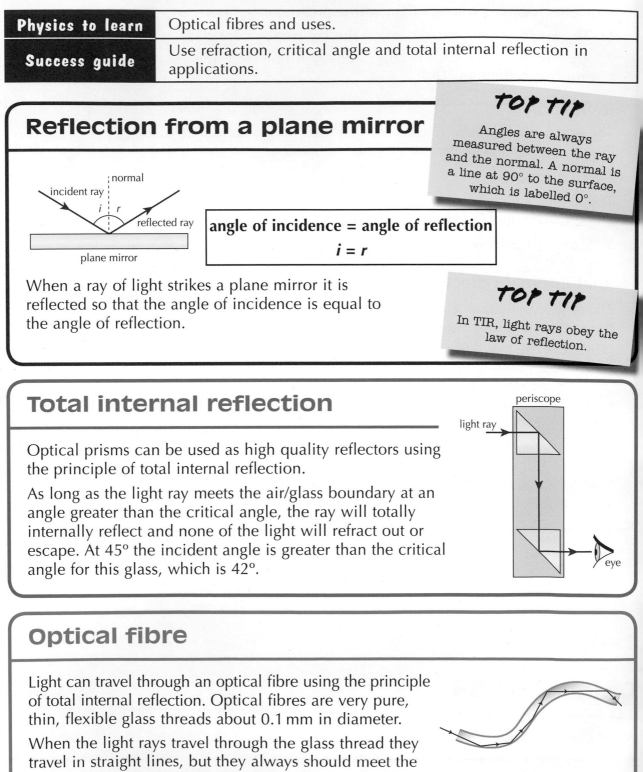

normal
incident ray
i   r
reflected ray
plane mirror

angle of incidence = angle of reflection

$$i = r$$

When a ray of light strikes a plane mirror it is reflected so that the angle of incidence is equal to the angle of reflection.

Total internal reflection

Optical prisms can be used as high quality reflectors using the principle of total internal reflection.

As long as the light ray meets the air/glass boundary at an angle greater than the critical angle, the ray will totally internally reflect and none of the light will refract out or escape. At 45° the incident angle is greater than the critical angle for this glass, which is 42°.

periscope
light ray
eye

Optical fibre

Light can travel through an optical fibre using the principle of total internal reflection. Optical fibres are very pure, thin, flexible glass threads about 0.1 mm in diameter.

When the light rays travel through the glass thread they travel in straight lines, but they always should meet the surface at an angle greater than the critical angle. The light travels by a series of total internal reflections. The optical fibre can be curved in gentle bends.

Applications of optical fibres

Optical fibres form the network of modern telecommunication systems.
An optical fibre can carry a signal from a transmitter (T) to a receiver (R):

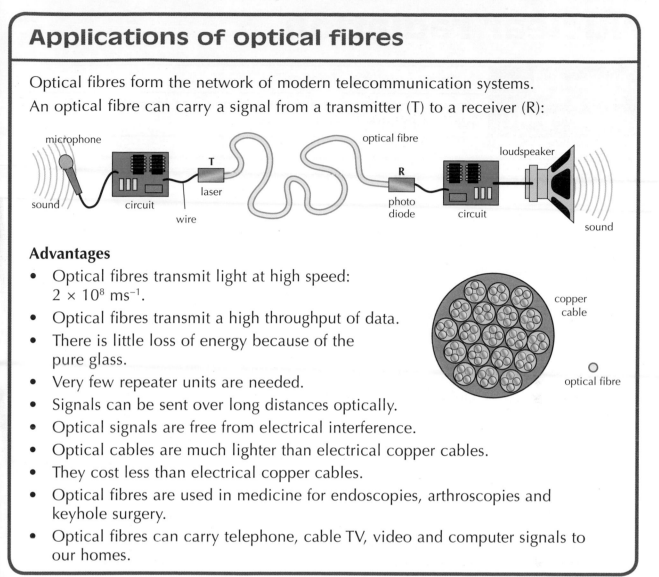

Advantages

- Optical fibres transmit light at high speed: 2×10^8 ms^{-1}.
- Optical fibres transmit a high throughput of data.
- There is little loss of energy because of the pure glass.
- Very few repeater units are needed.
- Signals can be sent over long distances optically.
- Optical signals are free from electrical interference.
- Optical cables are much lighter than electrical copper cables.
- They cost less than electrical copper cables.
- Optical fibres are used in medicine for endoscopies, arthroscopies and keyhole surgery.
- Optical fibres can carry telephone, cable TV, video and computer signals to our homes.

Quick Test 26

1. State the law of reflection.
2. What can be used instead of a mirror to reflect light?
3. What happens to light inside a periscope?
4. What invention transmits light through an optical fibre?
5. What is done to stop light escaping from the glass?
6. Give **five** advantages of an optical fibre over copper cable.

Nuclear radiation

Physics to learn	Nature of nuclear radiation.
Success guide	Know the structure of the atom, process of ionisation and nature of alpha, beta and gamma.

The atom

Atoms are the building blocks of elements and each element is made of only one unique type of atom.

Atoms have subatomic particles and all atoms have a nucleus at the centre with tiny electrons in orbit around this.

Nuclear radiation emits from certain nuclei and all the types of radiation we study here are called 'nuclear radiation'.

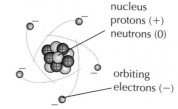

nucleus
protons (+)
neutrons (0)

orbiting
electrons (−)

proton

proton

neutron

hydrogen nucleus

uranium nucleus

TOP TIP

Atoms are neutral if the number of electrons = the number of protons.

The nucleus is made of neutrons and protons. Over 99% of the mass of an atom is in the nucleus.

Electrons are not part of the nucleus. They orbit the nucleus at certain levels with huge space between themselves and the nucleus.

The nature of radiation

There are three types of radiation emitted from the nucleus that we call nuclear radiation: alpha particles (α), beta particles (β), gamma rays (γ).

Alpha particles (α)

An alpha particle is made of two protons and two neutrons emitted from a large unstable nucleus. Alpha has two protons, therefore a positive charge of +2.

The mass of protons and neutrons is said to be 1 atomic mass unit or 1 amu each. This means the mass of an alpha particle is 4 amu. That is the heaviest of our three nuclear radiations.

Alpha particles are ejected from the nucleus at very high speeds: about 5–10% of the speed of light. However, they are the slowest of our three nuclear radiations.

Beta particles (β)

A beta particle is a very fast electron.

Beta particles are emitted from the nucleus when a neutron breaks up into a proton and the fast electron.

$$_0^1n \rightarrow {_1^1}p + {_{-1}^0}\beta$$

That electron is the beta particle. It has a lot of energy. Beta is a lot smaller than alpha. The mass of a beta particle is about 2000 times smaller than 1 amu or a neutron or proton. The beta particle has a charge of 1 and is negative, the same mass and charge as an orbiting electron.

The velocity of an ejected beta particle is faster than an orbiting electron.

Gamma rays (γ)

Gamma rays are bursts of energy that a nucleus emits to become more stable. On the electromagnetic spectrum these energy waves have a very high frequency and very short wavelength. Gamma rays have no mass or charge. Gamma rays travel at the speed of light. The speed of light is sometimes given as the symbol c.

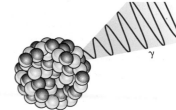

Velocity of gamma rays, $v_{gamma} = 3 \times 10^8$ ms^{-1}.

As well as being emitted from nuclear radiation on Earth, our sky is full of bursts of gamma radiation from the hottest and most energetic objects in the Universe. Our atmosphere absorbs gamma rays to protect us.

TOP TIP

Remember all these radiations are nuclear. Alpha and beta are particles; gamma is a burst or wave of energy.

TOP TIP

Remember the speed of light, c = 3 × 10^8 m s^{-1}.

Quick Test 27

1. State why an atom is normally neutral.
2. Where are the protons in an atom?
3. Which radiation is not a particle?
4. What is the charge on a neutron?
5. What charge is on an alpha particle?
6. What is the mass of a beta particle?
7. What does a gamma ray have?

Detecting nuclear radiation

Physics to learn	Activity, background radiation and ionisation.
Success guide	You can define activity. You can describe background radiation, ionisation and applications.

Activity

Radioactive decay takes place in a random manner. A radioactive substance contains many nuclei. We cannot say when any individual nucleus will decay, as the decay takes place at a random time, but with such a large number of nuclei in any sample we can observe the average number that are decaying in a certain time.

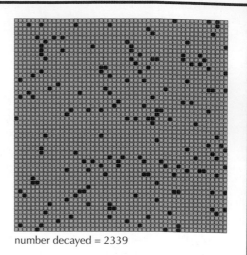

number decayed = 2339

This rate of decay is known as the activity of the substance:

$$activity = \frac{number\ of\ nuclei\ decaying}{time}$$

$A = \dfrac{N}{t}$

Activity of radioactive sources is defined as the number of nuclear decays per second, and is measured in becquerels (Bq). One becquerel is one decay per second.

Example

A sample of 1 g of uranium-238 has 720 000 decays in 1 minute. Calculate the activity of this source.

$$A = \frac{N}{t} = \frac{720\,000}{1 \times 60} = 12\,000\,Bq = 12\,kBq$$

Background radiation

Background radiation is all around us and has to be deducted from any measurements of radiation sources. We can count the radiation in becquerel (Bq). or measure the danger in Sieverts (Sv). Background radiation comes from two types of source: natural and artificial.

Most background radiation from natural sources comes from the radioactive gases around us.

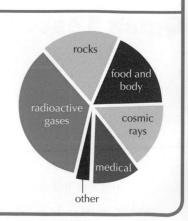

Natural source	Annual equivalent source (μSv)	Annual equivalent source (mSv)
Radioactive gases in air and buildings (radon and thoron)	800	0.8
Rocks of the Earth	400	0.4
In food and in our body	370	0.37
Cosmic rays from space	300	0.3
Total natural sources	**1870**	**1.87**

Most background radiation from artificial sources comes from the medical use of radiation.

Man-made source	Annual equivalent source (μSv)	Annual equivalent source (mSv)
Medical uses (X-rays)	250	0.25
Weapons testing	10	0.01
Nuclear industry (waste)	2	0.002
Other (job, TV, flight)	18	0.018
Total man-made sources	**280**	**0.28**

In addition to background radiation, annual effective dose limits have been set for extra exposure to radiation for the general public, and higher limits for radiation workers.

TOP TIP

The background radiation adds up to about 2 mSv per year per person.

Ionisation

Atoms are normally electrically neutral. Ionisation occurs when an atom gains or loses one or more electrons.

Adding an electron to an atom creates a negative ion with more electrons than protons.

Removing an electron from an atom creates a positive ion with fewer electrons than protons.

Ionisation can be caused by radioactivity. Alpha (α), beta (β), and gamma (γ) are ionising radiations as they can ionise atoms they hit. When ionising radiations collide with atoms they can knock an electron away, leaving a positive ion.

Alpha particles produce a much greater ionisation than beta particles or gamma rays. Alpha particles cause the most ionisation because they are the largest and because they have the greatest charge of the radiations. Alpha particles give up their energy quickest and are absorbed in the shortest distance.

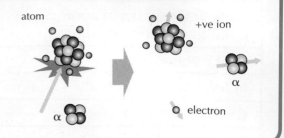

Absorption of ionising radiation

Radiation energy may be absorbed in the medium through which it passes. The absorption properties can identify the type of radiation.

A slow alpha particle cannot penetrate more than about 5 cm of air. Alpha is easily stopped by a few sheets of paper and cannot penetrate your skin. (Swallowing an alpha emitter is lethal as they don't escape the body.)

Fast beta particles can penetrate through several metres of air before losing their energy. Beta particles are stopped by a few millimetres of aluminium.

Gamma rays can penetrate the Earth's atmosphere. Air does not absorb gamma. They have very high energies. They can only be stopped by several centimetres of lead or several metres of concrete.

Alpha causes the most ionisation so has the least penetrating power.

Gamma causes the least ionisation so has the highest penetrating power.

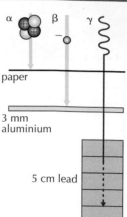

Identifying radiation

Alpha, beta and gamma radiations can also be identified by how they behave in electric or magnetic fields.

Deflection by magnetic field

In a magnetic field, charged particles are deflected. The alpha particles with a positive charge move in the opposite direction to the beta particles with a negative charge.

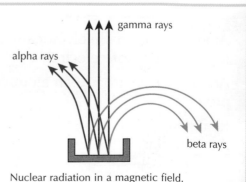

Nuclear radiation in a magnetic field.

The mass of the particles also has an effect on how far they are deflected.

Alpha particles have much more mass than beta and this makes them harder to deflect in a magnetic field.

Deflection by electric field

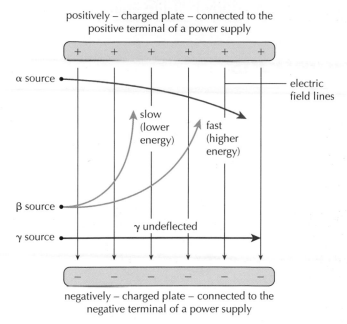

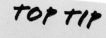

In an electric field, charged particles are also deflected. The alpha particles with a positive charge move in the opposite direction to the beta particles with a negative charge.

The mass of the particles also has an effect on how far they are deflected. Alpha particles have much more mass than beta and this makes them harder to deflect in an electric field.

Quick Test 28

1. Name **three** types of radioactivity.
2. Which type of radiation is a wave?
3. State what radioactivity does to atoms.
4. State which type of radioactivity is the most penetrating radiation.
5. State which type of radioactivity causes the greatest ionisation.
6. What happens to radiation energy as it passes through a material?
7. Name methods of distinguishing between the three types of radioactivity.

Measuring nuclear radiation

Physics to learn	Geiger counter and half-life.
Success guide	You can measure count-rate and measure half-life from experimental data. Create and study half-life graphs.

Detecting ionising radiations

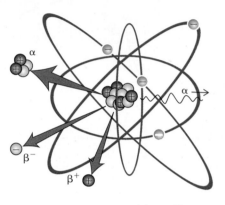

alpha and beta particles
and gamma photon

Nuclear radiations can be detected with a Geiger counter (above left). When in use we are not measuring the total activity of the source but are taking a sample measurement of the radioactivity that enters the Geiger-Müller tube of the counter.

This is recorded as a count rate and is measured in counts per minute or counts per second or becquerels (Bq). $1\,cs^{-1} = 1\,Bq$.

Activity and half-life

When a radioactive source emits ionising radiations [alpha (α), beta (β) and gamma (γ)] its nuclei are disintegrating or decaying and the source is changing into a different substance. The activity depends on the number of nuclei in the source: more nuclei = > more activity. The activity is the number of disintegrations occurring per second. The activity of a radioactive source decreases with time.

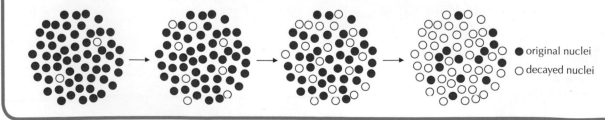

● original nuclei
○ decayed nuclei

As the nuclei disintegrate, there are fewer nuclei left to emit radiations.

The time taken for half the nuclei in a radioactive substance to decay does not change. This time is the half-life. The half-life of a radioactive substance is the time taken for the activity to drop to half its original value.

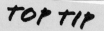

TOP TIP

The half-life time can be taken from any two points on a graph where the count rate halves.

Radioactivity is a random process. The decay of an individual nucleus cannot be predicted. The decay in activity can only be predicted because there are large numbers of nuclei in any sample. Different substances have different half-life times.

Nuclear medicine	Sodium 24	15 hours
	Iodine 131	8 days
	Cobalt 60	5.3 years
Carbon dating	Carbon 14	5760 years
Ageing rocks	Uranium 238	4500 million years

Measuring half-life

To measure the half-life of a source you will need:

- a detector of radiation, e.g. a Geiger-Müller tube and counter
- a stopwatch

1. First record the background count several times. Calculate the average and subtract this value from all readings.

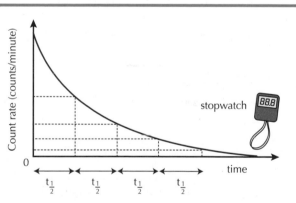

2. Place the source a fixed distance in front of the Geiger counter and record the count rate at regular time intervals.

3. Plot the count rate (corrected for background count) against the time taken on a graph.

4. Measure the time taken from any initial value of count rate on the graph to half this value.

5. The time for the count rate to keep halving stays the same. This is the half-life time.

Calculations

The fractional activity is useful in understanding how the activity changes with time.

Remember, a half-life has not taken place until the activity has halved: start with zero half-lives as shown in this table.

Number of half-lives	Activity (fraction)
Start = 0	1
1	1/2
2	1/4
3	1/8
4	1/16

TOP TIP

Most half-life questions are one of the three types of examples given on these pages. So study them well!

Example 1

Calculate the half-life of the source whose count rate has been recorded in the following table. The background count was recorded at 30 counts per minute.

Time (minutes)	0	30	60	90	120	150
Counts per minute	834	580	429	288	232	175
Corrected count rate (c/m)	804	550	399	258	202	145

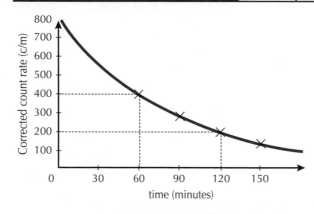

From the graph, the half-life of this source is 60 minutes.

Example 2

A source of activity 12 000 kBq has a half-life of four weeks. It is locked in a cupboard for 16 weeks. What is its activity after this time?

Activity	Number of half-lives
12 000	0
6000	1
3000	2
1500	3
750	4

Number of half-lives $= \dfrac{16}{4} = 4$

12 000 –> 6000 –> 3000 –> 1500 –> 750
      1   2   3   4

The activity after 16 weeks is 750 kBq.

Example 3

The activity of a radioactive source is 1600 MBq. 120 minutes later its activity is only 100 MBq. What is the half-life of the source?

Activity	Number of half-lives
1600	0
800	1
400	2
200	3
100	4

16 000 –> 800 –> 400 –> 200 –> 100
      1   2   3   4

There are four half-lives.

$\dfrac{120}{4} = 30$ minutes

TOP TIP

How many half-lives? Count the changes or arrows.

Quick Test 29

1. State the meaning of the term half-life.
2. What is needed to measure half-life?
3. Activity drops from 1200 Bq to 300 Bq in 30 minutes. What is the half-life?
4. A source with activity 2400 Bq has a half-life of 5 s. Calculate the activity after 25 s.

Using nuclear radiation

Physics to learn	Absorbed dose, equivalent dose, radiological protection and applications.
Success guide	You can understand dose measurements and how to stay safe.

Safety first

The early discoverers of radioactivity were not aware of its danger. Henri Becquerel first discovered uranium rays in 1896. At the same time, the husband and wife team of Marie and Pierre Curie were researching in Paris. Marie invented the word 'radioactivity' and discovered the radioactive elements polonium and radium in 1896–1900.

Radioactive elements are naturally occurring and they can be used in science and medicine. Too much radiation causes tissue damage, cancer, genetic disorders, and even death. Marie Curie died as a result of her research into and ongoing exposure to radioactivity.

Absorbed dose

When ionising radiation is absorbed by the human body, physicists can measure the energy put down by the absorbed particles and the mass of matter absorbing the radiation. From these, we can calculate the absorbed dose, which is the energy deposited per unit mass into the absorbing material. Gray (Gy) is the unit of absorbed dose.

$$absorbed\ dose = \frac{energy}{mass} \quad \boxed{D = \frac{E}{m}}$$

The gray, Gy, is the unit of absorbed dose.

One gray is one joule per kilogram: $1\,\text{Gy} = 1\,\text{J kg}^{-1}$

Example 1

A man has his whole body irradiated with alpha radiation until he has received 1 J of energy. Calculate his absorbed dose. Assume his mass is 80 kg.

$$D = \frac{E}{m} = \frac{1}{80} = 0.0125\,\text{Gy} = 12.5\,\text{mGy}$$

For comparison, a chest X-ray might deliver 0.3 mGy.

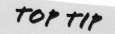

TOP TIP

Different materials will absorb different amounts of energy from radiation.

Radiation weighting factor

The absorbed dose measures the energy deposited in the tissue but does not take into account the effects of different types of radiation on the human body.

A radiation weighting factor (w_R) is given to each type of radiation as a measure of its biological effect. The higher the radiation weighting factor, the higher the biological damage on the human body.

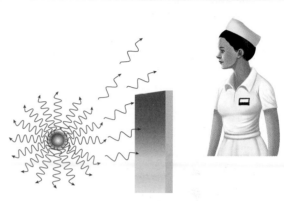

TOP TIP

The same dose of a different radiation can have a different biological effect.

Type of radiation	w_R
X- and γ-rays	1
β particles	1
α particles	20
Slow neutrons	3
Fast neutrons	10

Note, you do not have to remember these values as some will vary, e.g. with the energy of the particles. They will also be provided on the exam data sheet.

Equivalent dose

Equivalent dose combines the absorbed dose with the type of radiation. The equivalent dose (H) is the product of absorbed dose and radiation weighting factor.

Equivalent dose is measured in sieverts (Sv). $H = Dw_R$

The same equivalent dose always gives the same biological effect. For example, we now know that 1 mSv of γ radiation will do the same damage as 1 mSv of α radiation.

Example 2

The man in example 1 received his absorbed dose from alpha radiation, so his equivalent dose would be:

$H = Dw_R = 0.0125 \times 20 = 0.25 \, Sv$

Example 3

A nuclear industry operator receives an absorbed dose of 300μGy from slow neutrons and an absorbed dose of 4mGy from gamma radiation.

Calculate the total equivalent dose received.

We need to calculate the equivalent dose from each radiation separately before totalling:

Equivalent dose from slow neutrons

$$H_n = Dw_R = 300 \times 10^{-6} \times 3 = 900 \times 10^{-6} = 0.9\,mSv$$

Equivalent dose from gamma radiation

$$H_g = Dw_R = 4 \times 10^{-3} \times 1 = 4 \times 10^{-3} = 4\,mSv$$

Total equivalent dose

$$H = H_n + H_g = 0.9 + 4 = 4.9\,mSv$$

One not to worry over: due to Potassium-40, a banana gives you an equivalent dose of 0.1 μSv.

A further factor that affects the biological risk is the tissue type that the radiation is absorbed by. Doctors will study the tissue weighting factor if only a part of the body receives radiation.

Medical applications

When ionising radiation is used to treat cancer, the radiotherapy treatment is prescribed in units of Gy. When radiopharmaceuticals are used, they will usually be given in units of becquerel. Health risks are discussed in the sievert unit. Different units are used because they measure different things.

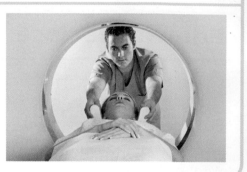

Radiological protection

Exposure to radiation can be harmful. The equivalent dose is reduced by shielding, by limiting the time of exposure or by increasing the distance from a source.

1. **Shielding:** Lead and concrete are good absorbers of radiation. A radioactive source is often kept in small lead cases. A radiographer will wear a lead-lined apron. Schools or hospitals will often keep their sources behind brick or concrete walls. A nuclear plant will make use of thick concrete round its reactor.

2. **Limiting exposure time:** Sources should be brought in and used in as short a time as possible.

3. **Increasing the distance from the source:** Radiation often spreads out like the rays of a light bulb. This means that intensity decreases rapidly with distance. Use tongs to increase the distance when in use. Just putting a source on the other side of the room when awaiting use may dramatically reduce exposure.

Quick Test 30

1. State what is meant by the activity of a radioactive source.
2. State what is meant by absorbed dose.
3. What is a radiation weighting factor?
4. What is equivalent dose?
5. What does the risk of biological harm from exposure to radiation depend on?
6. How do you reduce exposure to radiation?
7. Calculate the dose when 0.2 J is absorbed by 5 kg of tissue.
8. Alpha particles give a hospital worker an absorbed dose of 5 µGy. Calculate the equivalent dose.

Nuclear power

Physics to learn	Fission and fusion of nuclei.
Success guide	You can differentiate between fission and fusion. You can describe fission and fusion for generating power.

Nuclear fission

Fission is the splitting of a large nucleus. In fission, a nucleus with a large mass number splits into two nuclei of smaller mass numbers, usually with the release of neutrons. Energy is released.

Fission may be induced by neutron bombardment. An incident neutron can stimulate the fission of a nucleus with a large mass number. In the following reaction, the U^{235} momentarily becomes U^{236}, but this is unstable and immediately undergoes fission.

$$^{1}_{0}n + ^{235}_{92}U \rightarrow ^{141}_{56}Ba + ^{92}_{36}Kr + 3^{1}_{0}n + energy$$

slow neutron

$^{235}_{92}U$

$^{141}_{56}Ba$

$^{92}_{36}Kr$

Induced fission is used in the reactors in nuclear power stations.

Nuclear fusion

Fusion is the joining of nuclei. In fusion, two nuclei combine to form a nucleus of larger mass number. The nuclei that fuse together are usually very small. A large amount of energy is released, and no radioactive waste is produced in the reaction.

There is a virtually unlimited amount of the isotopes of hydrogen needed for fusion in seawater, and no greenhouse gases are emitted.

$$^{2}_{1}H + ^{3}_{1}H \rightarrow ^{4}_{2}He + ^{1}_{0}n + energy$$

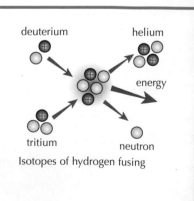

deuterium

helium

energy

tritium

neutron

Isotopes of hydrogen fusing

Nuclear fusion power stations

Fusion is the main energy process of the Sun and the stars, but physicists are working on the design of nuclear-fusion reactors for Earth! These experiments hope to provide the answer to the world's energy problems and be working by 2050. These international experiments are the biggest taking place on Earth.

TOP TIP

Nuclear fusion power stations are a good subject to research.

Nuclear power by fission

Today's nuclear power stations all use nuclear fission.

Advantages of nuclear power

- Nuclear power stations do not produce the greenhouse effect gases that thermal power stations do.
- Nuclear power does not need fossil fuels, which are in short supply.
- Nuclear power produces huge amounts of energy from very small amounts of fuel.
- Nuclear power stations produce small amounts of waste.
- Nuclear power is very reliable. Renewable sources depend on the wind and the Sun.

Disadvantages of nuclear power

- Nuclear power stations produce dangerous, radioactive waste. This waste has to be stored for a very long time.
- Uranium is a non-renewable fuel.
- There is a risk of radioactive material escaping from a nuclear power station in an accident.
- Nuclear power stations may be expensive to decommission when their useful life is over.
- Radioactive waste is the biggest problem for nuclear power. There is low-and medium-level waste, which can be treated in a similar way to dangerous waste from other industries. The high-level waste is more problematic. High-level waste can remain radioactive for thousands of years. The waste is carefully packed and stored in safe, stable rock formations.

The main parts of a nuclear power station are the nuclear reactor followed by a turbine and generator. The nuclear reactor uses fission of a fuel such as uranium to produce large amounts of heat energy. The heat is used to make steam to drive the turbine and generator. Electrical energy is produced.

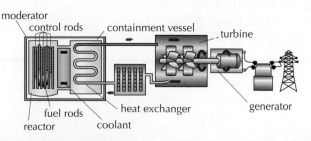

moderator
control rods
containment vessel
turbine
fuel rods
reactor
coolant
heat exchanger
generator

In the reactor, nuclear fuel (uranium) is bombarded with neutrons. Splitting the nucleus is the process of nuclear fission. The uranium 235 nucleus absorbs a neutron, then the nucleus splits

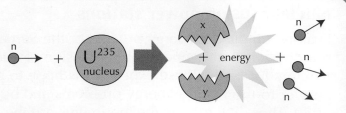

into two fission fragments plus two or three neutrons and a large amount of energy. This energy drives the power station.

In nuclear fission, the three neutrons released travel too fast to cause further fission, so in a nuclear reactor they are slowed first by travelling through a moderator. Control rods are also used to absorb neutrons to control the chain reaction.

A chain reaction

The neutrons released during fission can set off a chain reaction. Each neutron released can be made to cause a further fission reaction. The reaction needs to be controlled.

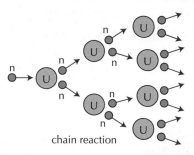

chain reaction

Fuel rods

Pellets of enriched (higher percentage) uranium fuel for fission are stacked in columns to make fuel rods. The mass of uranium in a rod is small (well below critical mass) so it will never cause an explosion. The rods are in groups to form a fuel element.

Moderator

Fast neutrons are emitted during fission. Fast neutrons are moderated (slowed) so that they can cause further fission. The fuel rods are placed in a moderator (graphite, water or heavy water). Neutrons from one fuel rod pass through the moderator and cause further fission in another rod.

Control rods

Electrical energy supply is maintained if one neutron from each fission reaction causes a further fission. This happens in a controlled chain reaction. Control rods made of boron can move in between the fuel rods to absorb neutrons. Rods can be partially raised to meet demand or fully put in place in an emergency.

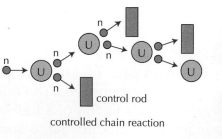

control rod

controlled chain reaction

Coolant

The heat produced in a nuclear reactor is removed using a coolant. The coolant can be a pressurised liquid or gas, e.g. water or carbon dioxide gas. The coolant then transfers its heat to water flowing through a heat exchanger. This water changes to steam, which can rotate the turbine.

Containment vessel

The core parts of a nuclear reactor are surrounded by a containment vessel (a steel lining and concrete). In the event of an accident the radiation, including gamma rays and neutrons, is contained. The containment vessel also protects the core from earthquakes and plane crashes.

TOP TIP

Discuss and debate whether you agree or disagree with nuclear power.

Quick Test 31

1. List the advantages and disadvantages of nuclear power.
2. What is nuclear fission?
3. Describe a fission reaction.
4. Name **four** parts of a nuclear reactor.
5. What is the problem with nuclear waste?
6. What is nuclear fusion?
7. Where might fusion reactions occur?

Scalars and vectors

| **Physics to learn** | Scalars, vectors, distance, displacement, speed and velocity. |
| **Success guide** | How to distinguish between terms, and add vectors. |

Scalars and vectors

We classify physical quantities as **scalar** or **vector**.

Scalars

A scalar quantity is defined by its magnitude alone. This means that it only has size. Scalar quantities are added using basic arithmetic.

Example

A lorry has a mass of 1500 kg and picks up a load of 500 kg. What is its new combined mass?

Just add them up!

1500 + 500 = 2000 kg

Vectors

A vector quantity is defined by both its magnitude and its direction.

Example

A basket and its load for a balloon flight have a weight of 5000 N. During the flight the balloon exerts a force up of 5000 N. What is the combined force?

If we just add the sizes we would obtain a value of 10 000 N. This is the wrong method! As one force is up and the other is down the forces should cancel each other out. The value will be 0 N so that the balloon neither rises nor descends.

TOP TIP

Magnitude is another name for size. Below are some examples of scalar and vector quantities.

Scalar	Vector
distance	displacement
speed	velocity
mass	weight
time	force
energy	acceleration
power	momentum

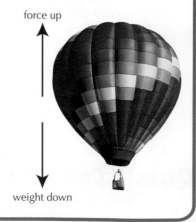

force up

weight down

Distance and displacement

Distance (d) is a scalar quantity.

It is defined by a number and its unit, the metre (m).

Displacement (s) is a vector quantity.

For example, a hiker walks 12 km due east from the village car park. Displacement is the distance travelled from a point in a certain direction. The direction may need some reference point, e.g. 30° east of north.

Speed and velocity

Speed is a scalar quantity.

The speed of an object is defined as the distance travelled per unit time (1 s).

Speed only has magnitude.

A speed limit of $20\,\text{ms}^{-1}$ does not need a direction.

Velocity is a vector quantity.

The velocity of an object is the speed in a given direction along a straight line. It is defined as the displacement per unit time (1 s).

Speed and velocity are measured in ms^{-1}.

A man walks along a conveyor belt in the opposite direction to the belt's movement. He is walking at a speed of $2\,\text{ms}^{-1}$. The conveyor belt is moving at a speed of $1.5\,\text{ms}^{-1}$. The velocity of the man over the ground is only $0.5\,\text{ms}^{-1}$ in the original direction.

Velocity is equivalent to speed with a given direction.

TOP TIP

We need to remember to state a direction when asked for displacement or velocity.

Quick Test 32

1. State what should be given to fully describe a vector quantity.
2. Give **two** examples of scalar quantities.
3. Give **two** examples of vector quantities.
4. Distinguish between distance and displacement.
5. Distinguish between speed and velocity.

Measuring displacement and velocity

Physics to learn	Displacement, average and instantaneous velocities.
Success guide	You can describe experiments to measure these quantities.

Measuring distance and displacement

Distance and displacement can both be measured with a metre stick or measuring tape. With displacement we must also give a direction. Displacement is taken to be the shortest straight-line distance from start to finish in a certain direction.

Distance

Path taken

Displacement

TOP TIP

The Latin word for distance is *spatium*, so we use *s* for displacement.

Measuring average velocity

Average speed is the total distance travelled over the total time taken.

$$average\,speed = \frac{total\,distance}{total\,time}$$

To measure the average speed of a cyclist on a road we could use a measuring tape and a stopwatch.

- Use the tape to measure a marked distance (e.g. 100 m).
- Use the stopwatch to measure the time taken (e.g. 6.5 s).
- Use the formula $\bar{v} = \dfrac{d}{t}$ to calculate the average speed as $\dfrac{100}{6.5} = 15.4\,\mathrm{ms}^{-1}$.
- Finally, to state the average velocity we need to note which direction the cyclist is travelling and add that to our description.

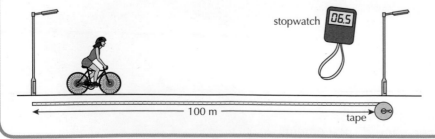

stopwatch **06.5**

100 m

tape

Measuring instantaneous velocity

Instantaneous speed is the speed at a certain time. A good estimate of instantaneous speed is obtained by using a very small time interval.

To measure the speed of a toy car a light-gate is attached to an electronic timer or computer timer.

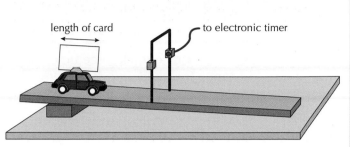

length of card   to electronic timer

A short length of card is attached to the toy car. The length of card passes through the light beam as the car moves down the slope.

- Use a ruler to measure the length of card.
- Use the light gate and electronic timer to measure the short time taken by the card through the beam.
- Use the formula $v = \dfrac{d}{t}$ to calculate the instantaneous speed at the light gate.
- To state the instantaneous velocity we could give the speed and state the direction as 'down the slope' or a similar statement.

Distinguishing average and instantaneous velocities

During a car journey, at different times the car increases speed, changes direction, decreases speed and occasionally stops.

The instantaneous velocity has to be calculated repeatedly.

The average velocity only needs to be calculated once from the total displacement and the total time:

$$average\ velocity = \frac{total\ displacement}{total\ time} \qquad \bar{v} = \frac{d}{t}$$

The displacement is the journey in a straight line from start to finish.

> **TOP TIP**
>
> List situations where instantaneous and average speed are different.

Quick Test 33

1. Describe how to measure displacement.
2. Describe how to measure average velocity.
3. Describe how to measure instantaneous velocity.
4. Explain why instantaneous speed changes.
5. How could you mark the difference between forward and backward?

Resultant vectors

Physics to learn	Resultant of two vectors.
Success guide	Can use scale drawing and mathematical methods with vector addition.

A runner goes round a race track three times. If the track has a length of 400 m, what is the runner's distance travelled and displacement?

Distance travelled: d = 3 × 400 = 1200 m.

Displacement is how far he is from the starting position. As he has returned to the start, displacement: s = 0 m.

Scale drawings

A vector can be represented as a line drawn to scale with an arrow to show the direction. To combine vectors:

1. Choose and write down a scale.

2. Add vectors drawn 'head-to-tail'.

3. Draw the resultant from 'start to finish'.

4. Measure both the magnitude and the direction.

Example 1

A walker walks 1000 m east before returning to a cafe 700 m back west.

Following the rules above, we can show the:

• scale: 1 cm = 100 m

• distance travelled: d = 1000 + 700 = 1700 m

• and the displacement: 1000 + (−700) = 300 m east.

Example 2

A sailor sets his boat on a heading of north at 5 ms⁻¹ through the sea.

The tide is moving at 2 ms⁻¹ in an easterly direction.

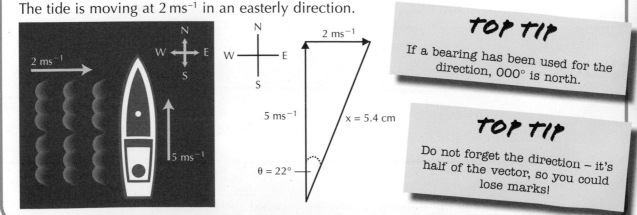

TOP TIP

If a bearing has been used for the direction, 000° is north.

TOP TIP

Do not forget the direction – it's half of the vector, so you could lose marks!

Find the boat's resultant velocity. As the vectors will be at right angles, you will have the option of using either a scale diagram or basic trigonometry.

1. Scale: $1\,cm = 1\,s^{-1}$.

2. Boat and tide velocities added on head-to-tail diagram.

   Resultant velocity, $v = 5.4\,ms^{-1}$ at 022°.

3. Resultant drawn start to finish.

4. a) Measured resultant, $x = 5.4\,cm$.

   b) Measured resultant angle, $\theta = 22°$.

Trigonometry

The mathematical rules

For size, use the Pythagorean theorem: $c^2 = a^2 + b^2$.

For direction, use trigonometric methods:

- $\cos \theta$ = adjacent/hypotenuse
- $\sin \theta$ = opposite/hypotenuse
- $\tan \theta$ = opposite/adjacent.

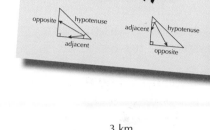

TOP TIP

Example

A car drives 4 km north then drives 3 km west. What is the resultant displacement?

Using Pythagoras and trig:

$$c^2 = a^2 + b^2$$
$$x^2 = 4^2 + 3^2 = 16 + 9$$
$$x^2 = 25$$
$$x = 5\,km$$
$$\tan \theta = \frac{3}{4}$$
$$\theta = \tan^{-1}\frac{3}{4}$$
$$\theta = 37°$$

displacement (s) = 5 km at 37° west of north. You can use a ruler and protractor to check this by scale measurement.

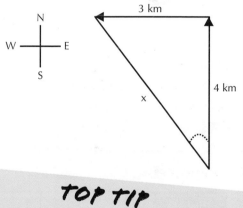

TOP TIP

$\tan \theta = \frac{3}{4}$ means you need to use the inverse function to find the angle. On your calculator find $\tan^{-1}$ or Inv tan. If you're getting, for instance, 0.01309 or 76.390 as your answer, you're not using your calculator properly!

Quick Test 34

1. State what should be given to fully describe a vector quantity.

2. A force of 90 N is exerted on a weight along a bench and a force of 30 N is exerted on the weight across the bench. Calculate the resultant force being exerted.

3. Two tugs pull on a boat with a force of 2 kN each and an angle between them of 90°. Calculate the size of the resultant force being exerted.

Velocity-time graphs

Physics to learn	Velocity-time on a graph.
Success guide	Can plot and interpret velocity-time graphs.

Plotting a velocity-time graph

Record the velocity of a moving object at regular time intervals.

Example 1

A ball bearing rolls down a grooved track from rest and its velocity is recorded every second for 6 s.

Time (s)	0	1	2	3	4	5	6
Velocity (ms^{-1})	0	0.1	0.2	0.3	0.4	0.5	0.6

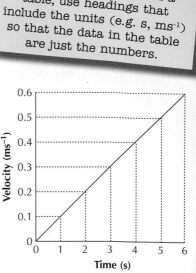

Example 2

A football manager paces along the touchline for 6 s at 2 ms^{-1} before taking 1 s to stop and turn around then returning at 1 ms^{-1} for 8 s.

Time(s)	0	1	2	3	4	5	6	7	8	9	10	11	12	13	14	15
Velocity(ms^{-1})	2	2	2	2	2	2	2	−1	−1	−1	−1	−1	−1	−1	−1	−1

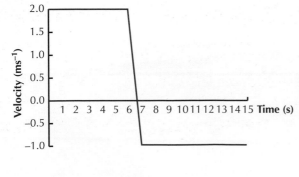

Why do the values become negative for the manager's walk?

As there is a change of direction we take forward to be positive and backward to be negative.

Interpreting graphs

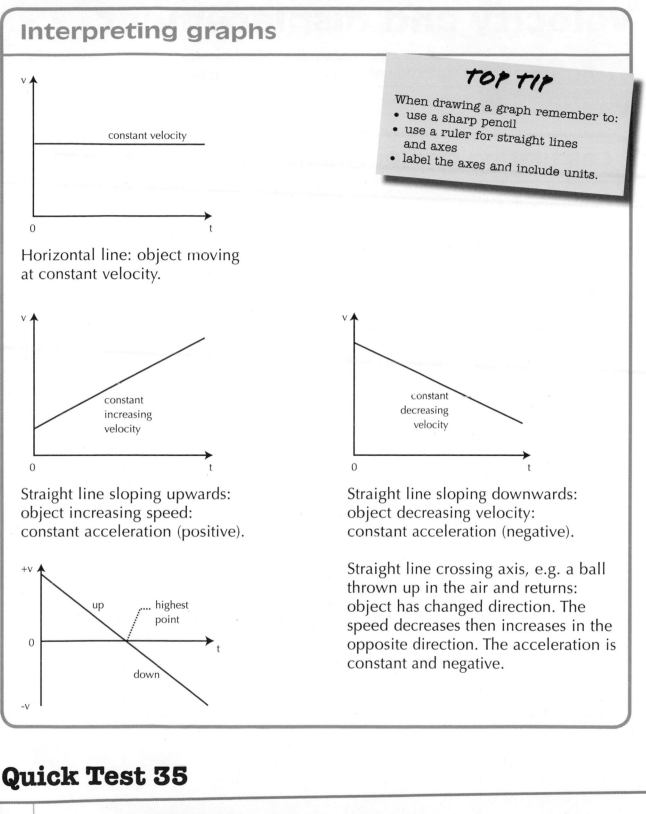

Horizontal line: object moving at constant velocity.

Straight line sloping upwards: object increasing speed: constant acceleration (positive).

Straight line sloping downwards: object decreasing velocity: constant acceleration (negative).

Straight line crossing axis, e.g. a ball thrown up in the air and returns: object has changed direction. The speed decreases then increases in the opposite direction. The acceleration is constant and negative.

Quick Test 35

1. What is the independent variable and where does it go?
2. What is the dependent variable and where does it go?
3. State what a change of axis signifies.
4. State what sensor can be used for time and velocity.

Velocity and displacement

Physics to learn	Displacement from a velocity-time graph.
Success guide	Can use a velocity-time graph to find an object's displacement.

Calculating displacement

Displacement is the distance travelled in a straight line from start to finish. Displacement is related to the average velocity by:

$$s = \bar{v}t$$

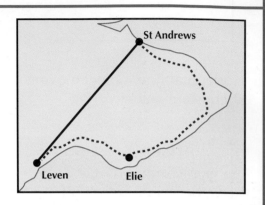

Travelling at constant velocity

A plane is flying at a constant velocity of $200\,\text{ms}^{-1}$ at 110° for 1 h 40 min.

The displacement can be calculated by formula:

$$s = vt = 200 \times (100 \times 60) = 1\,200\,000\,\text{m}$$

displacement = 1 200 km at 110°

The journey can be plotted on a v-t graph. The area under the v-t graph is the product of velocity on the y axis and time on the x axis.

Area = $200 \times 6000 = 1\,200\,000\,\text{m}$

The size of the displacement at 1 200 km is the same.

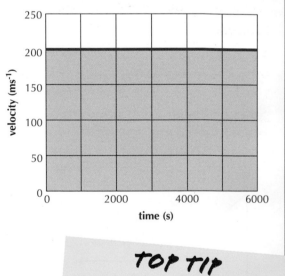

Displacement = area under a v-t graph

TOP TIP

The rectangular area is equivalent to l × b.

Displacement when accelerating

A racing car accelerates from rest to $100\,ms^{-1}$ in 10 s. Assuming it is constantly accelerating, draw a velocity-time graph and calculate the displacement required for this motion.

The equation:

displacement = area under a v-t graph,

can be applied when the motion is not constant. This is a useful alternative to the simple equation for displacement.

Displacement = area under a v-t graph

$$= (\frac{1}{2}(100 - 0) \times 10)$$

$$= 500\,m$$

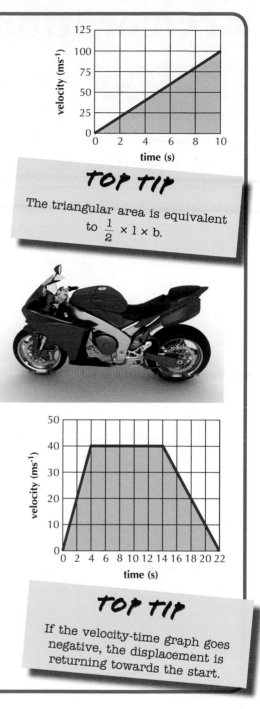

TOP TIP

The triangular area is equivalent to $\frac{1}{2} \times l \times b$.

Displacement on a journey

The type of motion on a journey varies. Divide the velocity-time graph into different areas. The total displacement is the sum of each area.

Example

A motorcyclist starting from rest accelerates to a speed of $40\,ms^{-1}$ in 4 s. He travels at this speed for 10 s before decelerating to a halt in 8 s.

Displacement = area under a v-t graph

$$= (\frac{1}{2} \times 40 \times 4) + (40 \times 10) + (\frac{1}{2} \times 40 \times 8)$$

$$= 640\,m$$

TOP TIP

If the velocity-time graph goes negative, the displacement is returning towards the start.

Quick Test 36

1. A car has to do an emergency stop. The car keeps constant velocity during reaction time. The brakes then operate to decelerate the car to rest.

    The car was going at $20\,ms^{-1}$, reaction time took 0.7 s and the car took a further 2 s to come to rest.

    Calculate the distance the car took to stop.

Acceleration

Physics to learn	Acceleration.
Success guide	Define and measure acceleration.

Describing acceleration

Acceleration (a) is the change of velocity in unit time (1 s). Acceleration is also defined as the rate of change of velocity.

$$acceleration = \frac{final\ velocity - initial\ velocity}{time}$$

$$a = \frac{v - u}{t}$$

$$v = u + at$$

My speed is increasing by 10 ms^{-1} each second. My acceleration is 10 ms^{-2}.

What is deceleration?

Acceleration is a vector. When the final velocity is less than the initial velocity, the acceleration will be negative.

A negative acceleration is a deceleration.

TOP TIP

For deceleration, use the acceleration equation. The answer is negative. An acceleration of −5 ms^{-2} is a deceleration of 5 ms^{-2}.

Example

A dog slows from 12 ms^{-1} to rest in 4 s. What is its deceleration?

$$a = \frac{v - u}{t}$$

$$a = \frac{0 - 12}{4} = -3\,ms^{-2}$$

The deceleration is 3 ms^{-2}.

Measuring acceleration

Acceleration on a slope

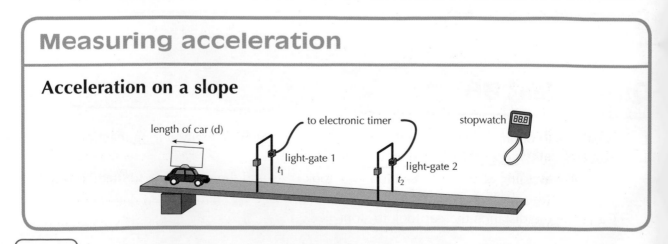

length of car (d)

to electronic timer

stopwatch

light-gate 1
t_1

light-gate 2
t_2

We can measure acceleration using two light gates and a stopwatch. We must obtain the velocity at two points on the slope and the time interval between them. A short measured length of card is attached to the vehicle to cut the light beam.

- At light gate 1 we use the length of card through light gate 1 and time t_1 to obtain an initial velocity, u. $u = \dfrac{d}{t_1}$

- At light gate 2 we use the length of card through light gate 2 and time t_2 to obtain a final velocity, v. $v = \dfrac{d}{t_2}$

- The stopwatch is used to record the time, t, between these two velocities.

- Then we can use the equation $a = \dfrac{v - u}{t}$ to calculate the average acceleration.

Acceleration at a point

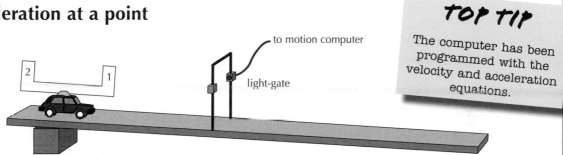

TOP TIP

The computer has been programmed with the velocity and acceleration equations.

to motion computer

light-gate

We can also measure acceleration using two cards and one light gate attached to a motion computer. This will find the acceleration at one point on the track. The second card cuts the light beam quicker than the first. The length of card must be measured and entered into the motion computer.

- Card 1 is timed and the computer calculates velocity, u, using the length of the card and time t_1.

- Card 2 is timed and the computer calculates velocity, v, using the length of the card and time t_2.

- The motion computer records the time between the two cards cutting the light beam and then calculates the acceleration, a.

Quick Test 37

1. State what is meant by the term acceleration.
2. What is a negative acceleration?
3. State what quantities need to be measured to calculate acceleration.
4. Calculate the acceleration of a car that increases its speed by 60 ms⁻¹ in 20 s.
5. A VW is travelling at 10 ms⁻¹ when it accelerates at 5 ms⁻² for 3 s. What is its new speed?
6. A bus is travelling at 20 ms⁻¹ when it decelerates at 2 ms⁻². How long does it take to stop?
7. A train slows from 35 ms⁻¹ to 20 ms⁻¹ in 5 s. Calculate its acceleration and deceleration.
8. Explain which method above would give the least accurate measurement of acceleration.

Acceleration graphs

Physics to learn	Calculating acceleration and gradients.
Success guide	Acceleration from a velocity-time graph.

Calculating acceleration

Calculating acceleration from a velocity-time graph

We can find the acceleration of an object by marking two points on a velocity-time graph and extracting data for the acceleration equation.

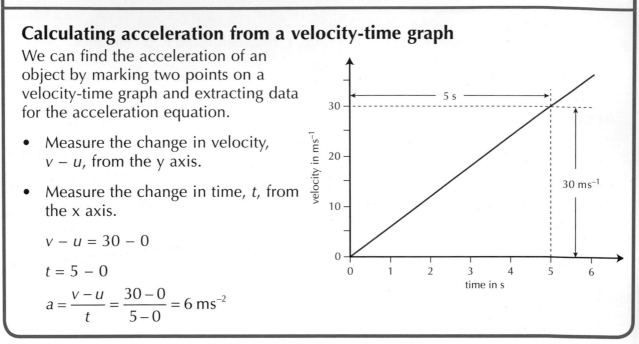

- Measure the change in velocity, $v - u$, from the y axis.

- Measure the change in time, t, from the x axis.

$v - u = 30 - 0$

$t = 5 - 0$

$a = \dfrac{v - u}{t} = \dfrac{30 - 0}{5 - 0} = 6 \text{ ms}^{-2}$

Gradients

Calculating acceleration from the gradient of a v-t graph

We can find the acceleration of an object by measuring the gradient of its velocity-time (or speed-time) graph.

$y_2 - y_1 = v - u$

$x_2 - x_1 = t$

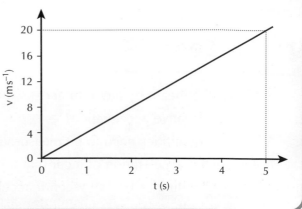

Example 1

The acceleration of the object in the graph is:

$a = \dfrac{v - u}{t} = \dfrac{20 - 0}{5 - 0} = 4 \text{ms}^{-2}$

Example 2

A motorcyclist starting from rest accelerates to a speed of $40\,\text{ms}^{-1}$ in 4 s. He travels at this speed for 10 s before decelerating to a halt in 8 s.

Check:

0 – 4 s:	$a_1 = 10\,\text{ms}^{-2}$
4 – 14 s:	$a_2 = 0\,\text{ms}^{-2}$
14 – 22 s:	$a_3 = -5\,\text{ms}^{-2}$

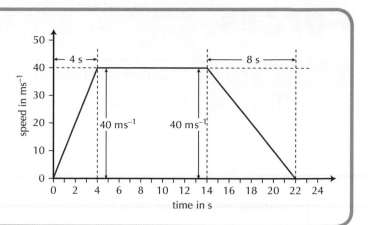

Identifying gradients

We can describe the acceleration from the gradient of a velocity-time graph.

On a velocity-time graph, if the line is horizontal and on the x axis then the velocity is zero and the object is stationary.

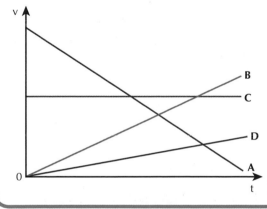

A = *constant deceleration*
B = *constant acceleration*
C = *zero acceleration*
C = *constant velocity*
D = *constant acceleration*
Note: the acceleration of B is greater than the acceleration of D.

Quick Test 38

1. State what the following show on a speed-time graph:

   (a) a horizontal line

   (b) a straight line sloping steeply upwards

   (c) a straight line sloping gently downwards.

2. Draw a speed-time graph to describe the following journey:

   A sprinter starting from rest accelerates to a speed of $10\,\text{ms}^{-1}$ in 2 s.

   He travels at this speed for the next 8 s then decelerates to $2\,\text{ms}^{-1}$ in 4 s.

   He continues to jog at this speed for the next 6 s.

Forces

Physics to learn	Balanced and unbalanced forces.
Success guide	You can use free body diagrams and explain the effect of friction.

Balanced forces

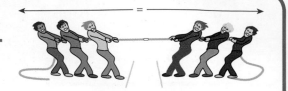

balanced forces: no motion

Force is a vector quantity. Force has size and direction.

Forces opposing each other may cancel out.
Forces that cancel out are balanced forces and there is no change in motion.

Balanced forces are of equal size but opposite in direction.

Unbalanced forces

thrust (T)
weight (W)

Forces applied to an object that do not cancel out are unbalanced.

Unbalanced forces cause acceleration.

The rocket experiences thrust from the engines but has weight from the gravitational field. Only if the thrust is larger than the weight will the rocket take off and accelerate.

Free body diagrams

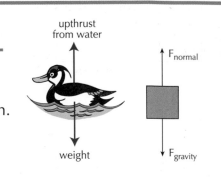

upthrust
from water

F_{normal}

weight

$F_{gravity}$

Free body diagrams can be used to show the forces acting on an object. A simple diagram is drawn and arrows are used to indicate the force and its direction. If one force is larger the arrow can be made longer to indicate this. The duck has weight, which acts downwards. The duck is not moving or sinking. The upthrust from the water must balance the weight.

Friction

Friction is a resistance force that opposes motion. When two surfaces run together, small collisions occur, which creates a force of friction. Friction increases as the velocity increases and the surface area increases.

Investigating the force of friction

Pull a shoe along at a steady speed. The pull has the same strength as the friction. A rougher surface would increase frictional force. A heavier weight would increase the downward contact force and therefore the frictional force.

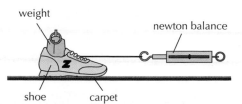
weight
newton balance
shoe   carpet

Increasing friction	Reducing friction
Increasing friction is useful to help an object speed up or slow down.	Friction should be reduced where it opposes desired motion.
• Dry tyres for racing cars have no tread to increase the contact area with the road.	• Streamlining of cars, cyclists, planes and bobsleighs reduces friction and saves fuel.
• Aerofoils push cars down at speed for better grip in the corners.	• Wheels, rollers and ball bearings are inventions designed to reduce friction and allow movement – roll not slide!
• Rough tarmac is laid before traffic lights.	• Hovercrafts use a cushion of air to reduce contact with the ground.
• A parachute has a large surface area for more air to hit.	• Machinery is lubricated. This reduces the contact between the moving parts.

TOP TIP
Weight down = the force of gravity down.

TOP TIP
Normal force is the force upwards from a surface.

Quick Test 39

1. Complete the following: Balanced forces are equal in _____ but opposite in _____.
2. Complete the following: Unbalanced force causes _____.
3. A book is at rest on a table top. Draw a diagram of the forces acting on the book.
4. A hammer falls to the surface of the moon. Draw its free-body diagram.
5. Name **two** methods of reducing friction.

Newton's first law of motion (N1)

Physics to learn	The first law.
Success guide	You know the first law and can explain relevant motion.

Isaac Newton

In 1687, Isaac Newton's book *Philosophiae Naturalis Principia Mathematica* or *Mathematical Principles of Natural Philosophy* made him one of the most important physicists of all time. As well as Newton providing important contributions to optics and calculus, his ideas on gravity and three laws of motion can still be used to explain the motion of most objects today.

Newton's first law

- An object at rest will remain stationary unless acted on by an unbalanced force.
- An object in motion will continue at the same speed in the same direction unless acted on by an unbalanced force.

Example

An aircraft is flying at a constant velocity.

- Constant speed: size of driving force = size of air resistance.
- Constant altitude: size of lift force = size of weight.

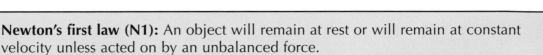

> **Newton's first law (N1):** An object will remain at rest or will remain at constant velocity unless acted on by an unbalanced force.

Newton's first law applies when there are no applied forces or the forces are balanced.

The motion remains the same.

Question: What should you do to keep an object moving?

Answer: Do nothing! An object should just keep moving, see N1.

On Earth we expect objects to stop. Newton says something must be doing the stopping. This is the force of friction acting between the object and the ground. Without friction the object would just keep going.

In space flight we can see the benefit of Newton's first law. Spacecraft cannot carry fuel for more than a few minutes of burn. In space, without friction, we can say there are no forces applied and objects will keep going without energy being used or the rockets being on.

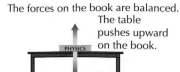

Stationary motion

The forces on the book are balanced.
The table pushes upward on the book.

PHYSICS

Gravity pulls downward on the book.

The book on the table could be said to be 'at rest'. Newton said there must be no unbalanced forces acting. We can see that there are forces acting but they are balanced. This is the same as no forces acting. Newton's first law says the objects will remain at rest.

Advanced thinking

Newton also knew that objects move with the Earth's rotation. So are 'constant velocity' and 'at rest' the same thing? Newton's first law says that whether you think the object is 'at rest' or at 'constant velocity', the object will keep its motion.

Constant velocity

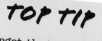

TOP TIP
- Don't forget that force is a vector.
- Balanced forces and no force give the same effect.
- The force of friction increases with velocity.

To keep a vehicle moving, we normally have to keep applying a force. Why is this?

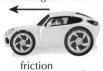
force of engine

friction

An object in motion experiences resistive forces that increase with velocity. These are known as the forces of friction.

Friction always acts against the direction of the motion.

Where the applied force and friction are balanced, Newton's first law tells us that the object will remain at constant velocity.

If the car is travelling at a higher speed then the engine force needs to be greater because the resistive friction forces have increased. The forces balance out again.

Frictionless motion

Friction is all around us and is often very useful. However, we may want to reduce friction to save energy loss. Here are some ideas to think about:

- The streamlined shape of a boat through the water reduces friction.
- A linear air track allows vehicles to float on a cushion of air in low friction experiments.
- The Maglev train might provide more transport for the future. Find out how the train uses repelling magnetic fields.

Quick Test 40

1. Describe the effect balanced forces have on the motion of an object.
2. Name a vehicle that keeps moving without requiring a force.
3. What outcome does Newton's first law have?
4. Describe what happens in a crash if you do not wear a seatbelt.
5. Why do we apply a force to keep an object moving?
6. What reduces friction for the Maglev train?

Newton's second law of motion (N2)

Physics to learn	Newton's second law.
Success guide	You know the second law and can explain relevant motion.

Acceleration and force

Unbalanced forces

The resultant of forces that do not cancel out is known as unbalanced force.

An unbalanced force causes acceleration. For instance, a racing car accelerates because its engine thrust is greater than the resistive forces. The difference in the opposing forces must be calculated.

Force, mass and acceleration

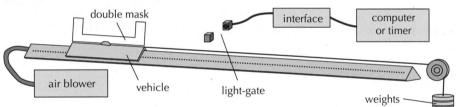

The air track reduces friction so it is not significant. The weights are applying a force to the moving system.

Experiment 1

The number of weights can be increased. The larger the force applied, the greater the acceleration. The acceleration varies with the unbalanced force.

This is called direct proportion: $a \propto F_{un}$

Experiment 2

The vehicle can have different masses. The larger the mass, the smaller the acceleration. The acceleration varies inversely with the unbalanced force.

This is called inverse proportion. $a \propto \dfrac{1}{m}$

Combining these conclusions: $a \propto \dfrac{F}{m}$

With mass in kg, acceleration in ms^{-2} and force in Newtons, this becomes:

$$a = \frac{F}{m} \quad \text{or} \quad F = ma$$

Newton's second law

> **Newton's second law (N2):** The acceleration of an object varies directly with the unbalanced force and inversely with its mass.

The newton is defined as the force that causes a mass of 1 kg to accelerate at 1 ms^2. Newton's second law tells us that an unbalanced force causes acceleration.

Example

An 800 kg car is on a gentle slope. The slope is just enough to balance out the effect of friction. The driver starts the engine and it exerts a force of 2.4 kN. Calculate the car's acceleration.

$$a = \frac{F}{m} = \frac{2400}{800} = 3\,\mathrm{m\,s^{-2}}$$

Example

A 900 kg vehicle accelerates. The engine force is 2 kN, but friction exerts 200 N. Find the acceleration.

$$a = \frac{F}{m} = \frac{2000 - 200}{900} = 2\,\mathrm{m\,s^{-2}}$$

Rocket launch

When a rocket launches:

- Liquid fuel engines (below the large central tank) are fired first.
- Thrust < weight. The rocket cannot accelerate or take off.
- Final checks are made and if there is a problem these engines can be shut down.
- If everything is OK, the solid fuel engines (the tanks on either side) are fired.
- Once ignited, these cannot be shut down and there is no going back!
- Thrust > weight. The rocket must take off, and it accelerates.

> **TOP TIP**
> Unbalanced force can be written as F_{un}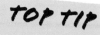

> **TOP TIP**
> Balanced forces are equivalent to no force and cause no change in speed or direction. Unbalanced forces cause change.

> **TOP TIP**
> Unbalanced force = applied force – force against friction.

Quick Test 41

1. What quantity increases acceleration?
2. What quantity decreases acceleration?
3. How can we find the size of an unbalanced force?
4. A 3500 kg boat accelerates at 0.5 ms^{-2}. Calculate the unbalanced force.
5. A toy car of mass 500 g accelerates at 0.6 ms^{-2}. If the friction is 0.8 N, what is the size of the pulling force?

Newton's third law of motion (N3)

Physics to learn	Newton's third law.
Success guide	Identify Newton pairs and apply the third law.

Newton pairs

In Newton's second law we saw the effect of a force on an object. But Newton noticed that when there is a force in action there is also another force in the opposite direction. We call these forces 'Newton pairs.'

Forces occur in equal and opposite pairs.

A Newton pair of forces has the following properties:
- These forces act on two different bodies at the same time.
- Both forces are of the same type (gravitational/electrostatic/magnetic).
- The forces are equal in magnitude.
- The forces are in opposite directions.
- The forces occur at exactly the same time, i.e. both objects will accelerate in opposite directions at the same time.

You push on a wall and the wall pushes you away.

Identifying Newton pairs

Here are various situations where you should be able to identify Newton pairs. For each diagram, try to write down the names of the forces involved.

TOP TIP

Two force sensors measure the forces. Can they have different values? No, if one person increases their force, both will experience an increased force.

Complete this sentence for each of the Newton pair diagrams.

The _____ exerts a force on the _____; the _____ exerts a force on the _____

Newton's third law

Newton said the forces of two bodies on each other are always equal in size but are directed in opposite directions.

TOP TIP

N3 tells us that forces exist in pairs.

Newton's third law(N3): If A exerts a force on B, then B exerts an equal but opposite force on A.

Newton's three laws and space travel

Newton's laws are used in space travel.

N3 tells us that forces exist in pairs: if the rocket exerts a force on the fuel, then the fuel exerts an equal but opposite force on the rocket.

rocket pushed forward

Thus, the fuel pushing on the rocket causes acceleration. N2 tells us that a force causes acceleration.

fuel pushed back

N1 tells us we need no force for an object to keep going. An object will remain at rest, or stay at constant speed in a straight line, unless acted on by an unbalanced force. Interplanetary flight takes place at a constant speed using no fuel.

TOP TIP

Newton's laws describe virtually all motion.

Quick Test 42

1. Use N3 to describe the Newton pairs when a toy water rocket is blown up and let go.
2. Describe the initial motion of the water rocket and what law applies.
3. What motion does the rocket then develop and why?
4. A girl pushes herself out of a boat of mass 160 kg, with a force of 400 N. Her weight is 600 N. Calculate the initial acceleration of the boat.

Newton's laws in action

Physics to learn	Applications of Newton's laws.
Success guide	You can apply the laws to car safety and terminal velocity.

Car safety

Seat belts and airbags

Consider objects in motion. N1 says that unless an unbalanced force acts, an object should keep its velocity. In a crash, if we are standing on a bus or do not have a seat belt on, Newton's first law says if no force is applied to us, we will just keep going forward at a constant velocity. We are not 'thrown forward'.

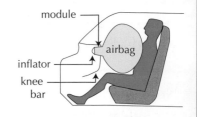

N2 shows that a seat belt applies a force in the opposite direction of motion, which decelerates the person with the vehicle. A seat belt will also have some 'give' so as not to cause injury.

A crash applies a large force in a short time. An airbag is designed to provide a longer time combined with a smaller force. The longer time is still only a fraction of a second but it can save your life.

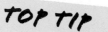

TOP TIP

A small force for a long time has the same effect as a large force for a short time.

Stopping a car

To stop a car, applying the brakes makes the tyres exert a force on the road again, and the road exerts an opposite force on the tyres, stopping the car. Without Newton's third law the car would not stop safely!

Terminal velocity

1. A skydiver initially accelerates downwards at $9.8\,\text{ms}^{-2}$ as the only downwards force is her weight.

2. As the skydiver's velocity increases, the air resistance increases and the acceleration is less. At a certain point in time she experiences air resistance of $600\,\text{N}$ upwards. If her mass is $70\,\text{kg}$, determine her motion at that point.

weight

Resultant force, F_{un} = total downwards force – total upwards force
$$= 686 - 600 = 86\,\text{N downwards}$$

Acceleration, $a = \dfrac{F}{m} = \dfrac{686 - 600}{70} = 1.2\,\text{ms}^{-2}$

3. Air resistance increases until it balances weight and a final constant velocity is reached (at about $60\,ms^{-1}$ without a parachute).

The final constant velocity of a moving object is known as **terminal velocity**.

When the skydiver opens the parachute, the greater surface area means a new lower terminal velocity will give the same air resistance to balance the weight, allowing the skydiver to descend safely.

> **TOP TIP**
>
> Air friction or resistance increases:
> • as the velocity increases and
> • as the frontal surface area increases.

Terminal velocity of a vehicle

> **TOP TIP**
>
> Better aerodynamics increases terminal velocity.

A. The driver presses the accelerator. The driving force makes the car accelerate.

B. The accelerator is kept down. Increasing air resistance => a smaller acceleration.

C. The accelerator is kept down. Air resistance now balances the driving force.

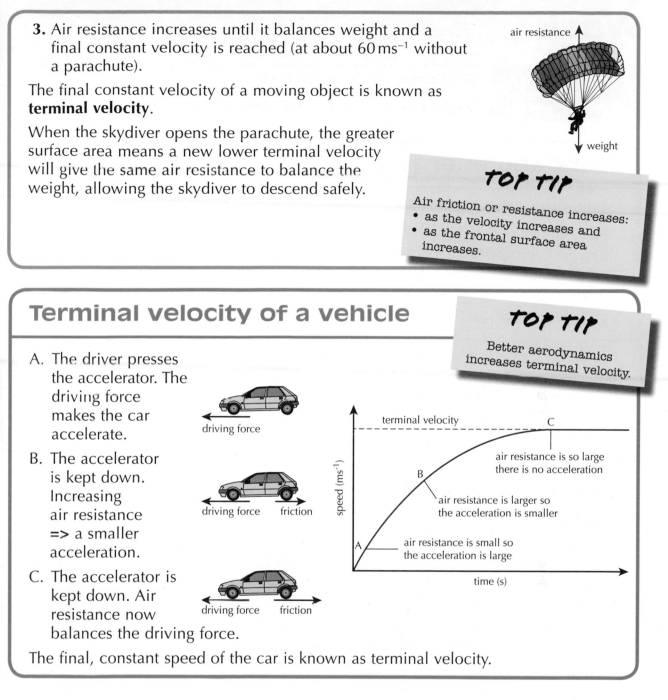

The final, constant speed of the car is known as terminal velocity.

Quick Test 43

1. Describe the effect of balanced forces on the motion of an object.

2. What does the size of the acceleration of an object depend on?

3. Why does a car have a top speed?

4. If a 2 kg block is pulled with a force of 10 N and friction is 2 N:

   (a) calculate the size of the unbalanced force

   (b) calculate the block's acceleration.

Work

Physics to learn	Work done, energy transferred.
Success guide	You can describe work done and its effect on displacement.

Work and energy

Work is done when energy is transferred to an object or energy is transformed from one type to another. Work and all forms of energy are measured in joules, J.

Work done is equivalent to energy transferred.

Work, unbalanced force and displacement

A force is said to do work when it acts on a body so that there is a displacement of the body in the direction of the force.

A swimmer pushes off a board to accelerate forward. Push is a force and work is done while the force is applied.

A weightlifter raises a set of weights above his head. If the weights are 1000 N he will have to exert a force of 1000 N in the opposite direction. Lifting a displacement of 2 m does twice the work of lifting 1 m.

2 m   1000 N

Here is an example of no work being done!

A person leans on and exerts a force on a wall. The wall also exerts a force on the person. As no displacement takes place, no energy has been transferred and so no work has been done.

Calculations

Work (E_w) is a scalar quantity, measured in joules (J).

We calculate the work done from the product of unbalanced force (F) and distance (d).

$$E_w = Fd$$

TOP TIP

Work done is an energy conversion. Work and energy are both measured in joules (J).

Examples

1. A workman exerts a force of 2.3 kN on a wheelbarrow over a distance of 180 m.

$$E_W = Fd = 2300 \times 180$$
$$= 414\ 000\,J$$
$$= 414\,kJ$$

2. A woman pushes her lawnmower a distance of 60 m and does 8 kJ of work.

$$E_W = Fd \quad 8000 = F \times 60 \quad F = 133\,N$$

3. When a car accelerates from rest to a high speed, the engine does work by exerting a large force during the distance travelled while accelerating. The work done changes to kinetic energy.

$$\boxed{E_W \rightarrow E_k} \quad \boxed{Fd = \frac{1}{2}mv^2} \text{ assuming no work is done against friction.}$$

In real life, friction is transferring energy to the surroundings. Some work is done against friction, and the rest becomes kinetic energy.

$$\boxed{F_{engine}d = F_{friction}\,d + \frac{1}{2}mv^2}$$

4. A girl lifts a vase from the floor onto a shelf a height of 2 m above the ground. The vase then slips and free-falls to the ground. What energy changes are involved?

During the lift work is done on the vase and the object gains potential energy.

$$\boxed{E_W \rightarrow E_P} \qquad \boxed{Fd = mgh}$$

During the fall the potential energy changes to kinetic energy.

$$\boxed{E_P \rightarrow E_K} \qquad \boxed{mgh = \frac{1}{2}mv^2}$$

Quick Test 44

1. A girl pushes her bike for 300 m with a force of 70 N. Calculate how much work she does.

2. A pupil weighing 500 N climbs the school stairs using 2500 J of energy. Calculate the height of the stairs.

3. A bag of weight 60 N is lifted onto a table of height 0.8 m. Calculate the work done and the potential energy gained.

4. A 1 kg ball leaves the player's foot at 30 ms⁻¹. How much kinetic energy did the ball gain?

Mass and weight

Physics to learn	Mass and weight.
Success guide	You can distinguish between mass and weight and identify gravitational field strength.

Mass

Mass is the amount of matter there is in an object. Mass depends not only on the size of an object but on what it is made from. (If it has a high density, it will have more mass.)

On the atomic scale, mass depends on the number and type of atoms.

Mass is scalar – it has only magnitude (size). We measure mass in kilograms (kg).

Gravitational field strength

An invisible field is said to exist around every mass, which we call the gravitational field. We say the field exists because we can see the effect of placing an object near a large mass such as the Earth. An object will accelerate towards the large mass. A mass requires a force to accelerate.

On Earth, the weight of every 1 kg of mass is 9.8 N. We can use 1 kg of mass as a fair test method of checking the field strength. The force (weight) on 1 kg of mass is measured. This weight per unit mass is equal to the gravitational field strength (g) and has the units $N\,kg^{-1}$.

The acceleration caused by gravity is numerically equal to the gravitational field strength.

On Earth the following apply: acceleration, $a = 9.8\,ms^{-2}$ and gravitational field strength, $g = 9.8\,N\,kg^{-1}$.

The gravitational field strength decreases as you move away from the surface of a planet or star.

For the first few kilometres from the Earth we do not notice the field strength drop much as the Earth is so much larger, but a spacecraft or satellite will observe the decrease in strength. Gravitational field strength is the force on unit mass. $g = \dfrac{F}{m}$

On Earth, 5 kg will weigh 49 N, $g = \dfrac{F}{m}$

$= \dfrac{49}{5} = 9.8\ N\,kg^{-1}$, i.e. 9.8 N on each kg.

TOP TIP

The larger the mass, the larger the strength of its gravitational field.

TOP TIP

You can look up the gravitational field strengths you need in the exam paper.

Weight

Weight is a force.

Weight acts downwards. Weight is a vector. Weight depends on both mass and the gravitational field strength. $W = mg$

Examples

A pile of rocks has been collected from the Moon. They contain 4 kg of matter.

On the Moon their mass is 4 kg and their weight is:

$W = mg = 4 \times 1.6 = 6.4\,N$.

Back on Earth, the rocks have the same 4 kg mass, but their weight has increased:

$W = mg = 4 \times 9.8 = 39.2\,N$.

TOP TIP

The mass does not change but the weight changes with gravitational field strength.

Planets

Objects in our solar system	Gravitational field strength on the surface (N kg⁻¹)
Earth	9.8
Jupiter	23.0
Mars	3.7
Mercury	3.7
Moon	1.6
Neptune	11.0
Saturn	9.0
Sun	270.0
Uranus	8.7
Venus	8.9

Example

An object weighs 150 N on Mars. What is its mass?

What would it weigh on the surface of Jupiter?

$W = mg \quad 150 = m \times 3.7$
mass of object, m = 40.5 kg
$W = mg = 40.5 \times 23 = 932.4\,N$

Quick Test 45

1. When g changes, does mass or weight change?
2. Calculate the weight of the following masses on Earth:
   (a) 750 kg   (b) 1×10^3 kg   (c) 450 g
3. Calculate the mass of the following weights on the Moon:
   (a) 32 N   (b) 9500 N   (c) 3 kN
4. Calculate the weight of 1000 kg on Mercury.

Projectile motion

Physics to learn	Projectile motion and applications.
Success guide	You can explain and do calculations on projectile motion.

Projectiles from space

Projectile motion occurs once an object has been put into motion by a force and then the only force acting on it is the force of gravity. The path of the projectile is known as its **trajectory**.

Consider a space vehicle before it re-enters our atmosphere.

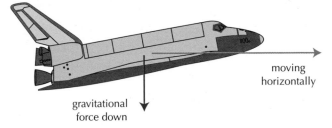

gravitational force down

moving horizontally

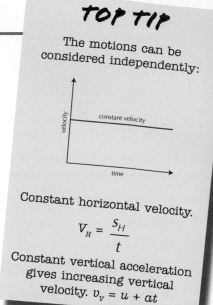

TOP TIP

The motions can be considered independently:

constant velocity

Constant horizontal velocity.

$$V_H = \frac{s_H}{t}$$

Constant vertical acceleration gives increasing vertical velocity. $v_V = u + at$

Assume no friction acting.

The space vehicle is travelling horizontally at a constant velocity.

The force of gravity pulls on the space vehicle in a vertically downwards direction. The force of gravity creates acceleration downwards.

The resultant velocity at any point in the trajectory is a combination of both the constant horizontal velocity and the increasing vertical velocity at that point.

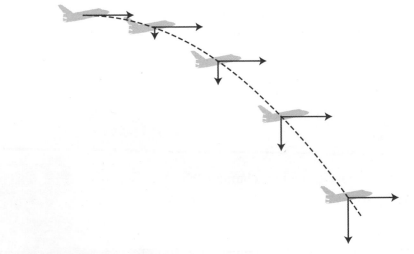

The space vehicle follows a projectile trajectory.

Projectiles fired horizontally

What is important to remember is that the motion along the horizontal direction does not affect the motion along the vertical direction and vice versa. Horizontal motion and vertical motion are totally independent of each other.

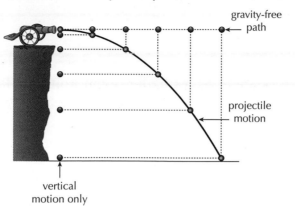

- The horizontal motion remains constant velocity.
- The vertical motion is constant acceleration.

Example

A ball is falling off a cliff with a velocity of $7\,ms^{-1}$. It is in flight for 3s.

What range does it have?
What is the resultant velocity on impact?

Horizontally:

$V_H = 7\,ms^{-1}$ $t = 3s$

$d_H = vt = 7 \times 3 = 21\,m$

Range = 21m

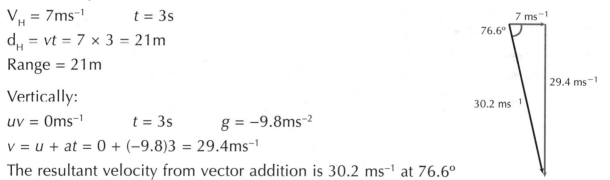

Vertically:

$uv = 0\,ms^{-1}$ $t = 3s$ $g = -9.8\,ms^{-2}$

$v = u + at = 0 + (-9.8)3 = 29.4\,ms^{-1}$

The resultant velocity from vector addition is $30.2\ ms^{-1}$ at $76.6°$

Quick Test 46

1. State what forces are acting on a projectile.
2. State the direction of that force.
3. What is the direction of the acceleration?

Satellites

Physics to learn	Newton's thought experiment and satellites.
Success guide	You can explain satellite orbits.

Satellites

A satellite is usually thought of as a smaller body orbiting a larger body. Satellites can be divided into two groups: natural satellites and artificial satellites.

Natural satellites

Moons are natural satellites. A natural satellite orbits a planet or other celestial object.

Artificial satellites

An object that has been put into space by human effort is an artificial satellite.

The first artificial artificial ever launched was the Sputnik 1 from the Soviet Union in 1957. Since then, over 8000 artificial satellites have been launched, although most of these are now space debris.

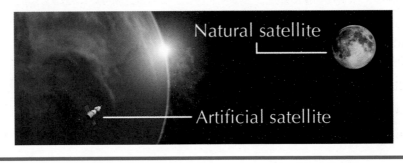

Newton's thought experiment

Why does the apple fall to the ground but the Moon stay in orbit?

Isaac Newton used the idea of a cannonball being fired from the top of a very high mountain and parallel to the Earth.

If there was no gravity, then the cannonball should follow a straight line away from Earth.

However, Newton knew that a cannonball would normally follow a projectile trajectory. If the initial velocity was increased, Newton illustrated the increased path that the cannonball would take.

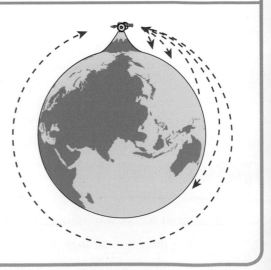

Satellite motion extends the ideas of projectile motion.

Satellite motion was first predicted by Newton in his **thought experiment** over 300 years ago.

TOP TIP

Research Newton's thoughts on gravity and the planets.

Newton thought if a cannonball was fired off a very high mountain fast enough it would never reach the ground. Instead it would remain in free-fall towards the Earth but, because the Earth is round, the cannonball would remain in orbit as an artificial satellite.

The apple falls to the ground and satellites remain in orbit because of the same gravitational force.

Satellite orbits

Today satellites are launched into orbit in space at great heights. Earth's mountains are not high enough!

The highest mountain on Earth is Mount Everest, at 8848 m, which is nearly 9 km.

Orbits for useful satellites are much higher than this. TV satellites in geo-stationary orbit are found at 36 000 km.

TOP TIP

The Earth has a radius of about 6000 km.

Low Earth orbit is up to 2000 km.

Medium Earth orbit is from 2000 to 36 000 km.

High Earth orbit is above 36 000 km.

Quick Test 47

1. What sensation do you experience in free-fall?
2. In which direction does a projectile have:
   (a) constant speed?
   (b) acceleration?
3. How can a satellite be projected into orbit?
4. Write out a definition of a natural and an artificial satellite.
5. At what height are the two boundaries between the different orbit bands?

Space exploration

Physics to learn	Telescopes and the Universe.
Success guide	Describe how telescopes and space exploration show us the Universe.

An astronomical telescope

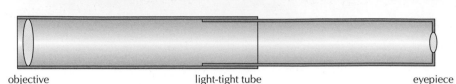

objective lens   light-tight tube (moves to focus)   eyepiece lens

The first telescopes were developed from 1608.

The **objective** lens has a large diameter to collect many light rays for a brighter image. The lens has a long focal length and produces an inverted image inside the tubes, near to the eyepiece lens.

The **eyepiece** lens magnifies the image. The eyepiece has a small diameter, as the eye pupil is small. The combined telescope result is virtual, inverted and magnified.

Telescopes for the Universe

Information about astronomical objects comes from observing visible light and also from space telescopes and observatories, which are used to detect radiations from the different parts of the electromagnetic spectrum.

Gamma ray

The Fermi Gamma-ray Space Telescope detects shortwave gamma rays, which are emitted by neutron stars, pulsars and black holes.

X-ray

The Chandra X-ray Observatory detects even faint X-rays.

Ultraviolet, visible, infrared

The Hubble space telescope carries telescopes for detecting ultraviolet, visible and infrared radiations. Spitzer is an older infrared telescope.

Microwave

The Planck telescope plots microwave background radiation.

Radio

Radio telescopes can be used singly or in an array.

Further detection

Telescopes also detect cosmic particles and in future telescopes will search for gravitational waves.

The Universe

Cosmic microwave background radiation and cosmic infrared radiation give us different insights into our Universe.

Re-entry risks

Materials on a spacecraft cannot be allowed to melt or change state on re-entry to the earth's atmosphere. Special silica tiles may be used to absorb the heat.

The amount of energy that can change the state of a material varies with:

- the mass of material being heated $(E \propto m)$
- the specific latent heat of the material to be used $(E \propto l)$

$$E = ml \qquad l = \frac{E}{m} \qquad m = \frac{E}{l}$$

From solid to liquid, l is the latent heat of fusion, l_f.
From liquid to gas, l is the latent heat of vaporisation, l_v.

Quick Test 48

1. In the telescope, which lens has the longest focal length?
2. Which telescope lens has the larger diameter?
3. List different radiations detected from space.
4. In what spectrum can different telescopes detect radiations?
5. Is a radio telescope a detector of long or short wavelengths?

Cosmology

Physics to learn	Light years, the Universe and space telescopes.
Success guide	You can convert light years to metres, and show how telescopes reveal the Universe.

Light years

Distances are so vast in space that astronomers use a unit for distance called the light year.

1 light year = the distance travelled by light in 1 year.

You can calculate how far this distance is in metres using $d = vt$.

$$d = vt = (3 \times 10^8) \times (1 \times 365 \times 24 \times 60 \times 60)$$
$$= 9.46 \times 10^{15} \, \text{m}$$

Here are some approximate distances:

Earth to Moon	1.2 light seconds
Earth to Sun	500 light seconds (8 minutes)
Our Sun to the next star	4.3 light years
Across our galaxy	100 000 light years

The closest star to our Sun is 24 million million miles away. That is 38 000 000 000 000 km. To measure the distance as 4.3 light years is more practical.

When our Sun goes below the horizon, it actually did so 8 minutes ago!

Modern space probes and the Planck telescope have provided data which has been used to calculate the age of the Universe – about 13.8×10^9 years or 13.8 billion years.

the rest of the universe
(invisible to us)

visible universe

Light took 14 billion light years to travel but due to expansion of the universe, objects are now 46 billion light years away.

TOP TIP

A light year sounds like a time but we must remember this is a distance!

TOP TIP

Time must be in seconds to work out distance in metres for a light year.

The observable Universe

A Solar System consists of a star and, in orbit around it, planets, moons, asteroids and comets. Our star, the Sun, contains over 99% of the mass of our Solar System.

Earth is one of eight planets: Mercury, Venus, Earth, Mars, Jupiter, Saturn, Uranus and Neptune. Four of these planets are small and rocky, then there is the asteroid belt, then four giant planets made of gas. Pluto is a dwarf planet.

Here is a memory aid for the order of the planets:
My **V**ery **E**xcellent **M**um **J**ust **S**erved **U**s **N**achos.
Our Solar System is a tiny part of the Universe.

TOP TIP

In the Big Bang theory, red shift and cosmic microwave background radiation suggests that the Universe is expanding and has a beginning.

Planet	A natural satellite of the Sun.
Moon	A natural satellite of a planet.
Sun	A star (one of 100 000 million in our galaxy!)
Star	Emits light and heat radiation.
Solar System	The Sun and the objects that orbit it.
Exoplanet	A planet orbiting a star other than our own Sun.
Galaxies	Consist of millions of stars.
Universe	Contains billions of galaxies.

From the electromagnetic spectrum

Information about astronomical objects is gathered using all the bands of the electromagnetic spectrum. All these radiations travel through space at 3×10^8 ms^{-1}.

However, the atmosphere absorbs these radiations by different amounts.

There are radio, microwave and visible telescopes on Earth, perhaps some on high mountains in countries with clear skies, but many of the latest telescopes are now put in orbit so that higher resolution can be obtained, so we can delve further into space.

Remember the order of the electromagnetic spectrum:
* Gamma rays have the shortest wavelength, highest frequency and most energy
* X-rays
* Ultraviolet
* Visible spectrum = ROYGBIV
* Infrared
* Microwave
* Radio waves have the longest wavelength, lowest frequency and least energy

a radio telescope

Quick Test 49

1. Calculate the distance in metres that light travels in 1 minute.
2. Calculate the distance of a light year in metres and in scientific notation.
3. Describe an exoplanet.
4. What is the name for a group of stars?
5. What absorbs radiation from space?
6. What radiation has the lowest frequency in the electromagnetic spectrum?

Quick Test 29

1. Time taken for the activity to drop to half its original value
2. Stopwatch and detector
3. 15 minutes
4. 75 Bq

Quick Test 30

1. The activity, A, of a radioactive source is the number of decays per second; $A = Nt$. The activity of a radioactive source is measured in becquerels (Bq); one becquerel is one decay per second.

2. The absorbed dose, D, is the energy absorbed per unit mass of the absorbing material; $D = \dfrac{E}{m}$.

   The gray, Gy, is the unit of absorbed dose; one Gy is equal to one joule per kilogram $1\,Gy = 1\,J\,kg^{-1}$

3. A radiation weighting factor, w_R, is given to each type of radiation as a measure of its biological effect.

4. The equivalent dose, H, is the product of absorbed dose, D, and radiation weighting factor w_R; equivalent dose H is measured in sieverts, Sv $H = Dw_R$

5. The absorbed dose; the kind of radiation; the body organs or tissue exposed

6. Shielding, limit time and increase distance

7. $D = \dfrac{E}{m} = \dfrac{0.2}{5} = 0.04\,Gy$

8. $H = Dw_R = 5 \times 10^{-6} \times 20 = 100 \times 10^{-6} = 100\,\mu Sv$

Quick Test 31

1. See page 84 for lists of the advantages and disadvantages of nuclear power
2. Splitting of nucleus
3. Neutron absorbed by nucleus which breaks into smaller parts and releases energy
4. Any four: fuel rods, moderator, control rods, coolant, containment vessel
5. It is radioactive
6. Joining of light nuclei into one with larger mass number
7. Stars or new experimental power stations

Quick Test 32

1. Magnitude and direction
2. Any two from: distance, speed, mass, time, energy
3. Any two from: displacement, velocity, weight, force, acceleration
4. Displacement = distance + direction
5. Velocity = speed + direction

Quick Test 33

1. Distance from start to finish with tape; note direction
2. Measure total distance travelled; measure total time taken; calculate using $\bar{v} = \dfrac{d}{t}$
3. Measure a very short distance; time this short distance; calculate using $\bar{v} = \dfrac{d}{t}$; see page 93 for more detail
4. Instantaneous speed varies at different points in time
5. Use positive and negative for vectors

Quick Test 34

1. Size and direction
2. 95 N at 18° from line of bench
3. 2.8 kN

Quick Test 35

1. Time, x-axis
2. Velocity, y-axis
3. Change of direction
4. Ultrasound

Quick Test 36

1. 34 m

Quick Test 37

1. Acceleration is the change in velocity in unit time
2. Deceleration
3. Distance, time × 3
4. $3\,\text{ms}^{-2}$
5. $25\,\text{ms}^{-1}$
6. 10 s
7. $-3\,\text{ms}^{-2}$ and $3\,\text{ms}^{-2}$
8. Using the stopwatch by hand gives the greatest uncertainty in the measurement of acceleration

Quick Test 38

1. (a) Constant speed
   (b) Large constant acceleration
   (c) Small constant deceleration

2.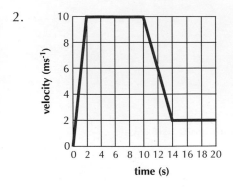

Quick Test 39

1. Size, direction
2. Acceleration

3.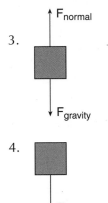

4.

5. Streamlining, lubrication

Quick Test 40

1. They have no effect
2. Spacecraft
3. No change in motion
4. You just keep going
5. To balance the force of friction
6. Magnetic fields

Quick Test 41

1. Unbalanced force
2. Mass
3. Difference in opposing forces
4. 1750 N
5. 1.1 N

Quick Test 42

1. The rocket puts a force on the water, the water puts an opposite force on the rocket
2. Acceleration, N2
3. Constant velocity because of N1 and air resistance
4. $2.5 \, ms^{-2}$

Quick Test 43

1. No overall effect
2. Mass of object, size of force
3. Air resistance balances engine force
4. (a) 8 N

   (b) $4 \, ms^{-2}$

Quick Test 44

1. 21 000 J
2. 5 m
3. 48 J and 48 J
4. 450 J

Quick Test 45

1. Weight changes
2. (a) 7500 N

   (b) 1×10^4 N

   (c) 4.50 N
3. (a) 20 kg

   (b) 5937.5 kg

   (c) 1875 kg
4. 3700 N

Quick Test 46

1. Only the force of gravity
2. Downwards
3. Downwards

Quick Test 47

1. Weightlessness
2. (a) horizontal

   (b) vertical
3. High and fast
4. Natural satellite: A natural satellite orbits a planet or other celestial object, e.g. a moon. Artificial satellite: An object that has been put into space by human effort.
5. 2000 km; 36 000 km

Quick Test 48

1. The objective
2. The objective
3. For example: gamma, X-ray, ultraviolet, visible, microwave, radio
4. Electromagnetic
5. Long

Quick Test 49

1. 1.8×10^{10} m
2. 9.46×10^{15} m
3. A planet orbiting a star other than our own Sun
4. Galaxy
5. The atmosphere
6. Radio waves

Quick Test 50

1. Refraction and diffraction
2. Each type of atom has its own set of electrons
3. Line spectra
4. Red, orange, yellow, green, blue, indigo, violet
5. Atom